UNAFRAID

UNAFRAID

MOVING
BEYOND
FEAR-BASED
FAITH

BENJAMIN L.
COREY

HarperOne
An Imprint of HarperCollinsPublishers

HarperOne

HarperCollins books may be purchased for educational, business, or sales promotional use. For information, please email the Special Markets Department at SPsales@harpercollins.com.

FIRST HARPERCOLLINS PAPERBACK EDITION PUBLISHED IN 2019

Designed by SBI Book Arts, LLC

Library of Congress Cataloging-in-Publication Data is available upon request.

ISBN 978-0-06-247160-4

19 20 21 22 23   LSC   10 9 8 7 6 5 4 3 2 1

For God did not give us the spirit of fear, but
one of power and love . . .

—2 Timothy 1:7

CONTENTS

1.

A SPIRITUAL MIDLIFE CRISIS

On January 3, 2015, the Islamic State of Iraq and Syria (ISIS) posted one of its trademark execution videos online. ISIS fighters executed Muath al-Kasasbeh, a Jordanian pilot who had been captured after his fighter jet crashed during a United States–led airstrike over Syria; and they did it the way the Catholic Church and John Calvin once had: by burning him alive. In defiance of both the Qur'anic prohibition of taking innocent life and the teachings of the Prophet Muhammad, these soldiers placed al-Kasasbeh inside a metal cage, doused him with flammable liquid, set him on fire, and filmed his grisly death.

The outrage across the globe was swift and just. The Jordanian government called the execution by fire "vile" and promised to harshly retaliate, while the president of the United States called the execution "depraved."[1] Christians, of course, were among those to decry the burning of al-Kasasbeh, and rightly so. However, as I listened to the righteous indignation of my Christian brothers and sisters, I quickly became aware of a glaring blind spot that many didn't seem to even notice: our mental image of God was shockingly similar to the ISIS terrorists who burned al-Kasasbeh alive.

You see, that Jordanian pilot was a Muslim; and according to the flavor of Christian theology that many of us grew up with, as a Muslim he was not "saved" and thus was destined for hell after his death—a place where, you guessed it, he would be burned alive forever and ever in eternal conscious torment. As I watched my fellow Christians express outrage and disgust over his burning in this life, I kept thinking to myself, "You guys—you realize that you believe God is going to do this to the vast majority of people who have ever lived, *don't you*?"

Think about that for a minute: if the theology of salvation and hell that so many of us grew up with is true, the moment that Muslim pilot succumbed to the flames and died, he immediately went to a place where the flames and torture started *all over again.* According to the traditional hellfire theology, al-Kasasbeh went from twenty-two minutes of burning alive to an e-freaking-ternity of burning alive—with *no hope of even death to stop the torment.* Essentially, to affirm the hellfire theology of my youth, a person would say that what God did to al-Kasasbeh after death is *far worse and less unmerciful than what ISIS did to him.* If the traditional theology of hell is correct, God is like an ISIS terrorist—but like one on steroids.

If it is depraved and disgusting when ISIS does it, why is it good and just when God does it?

Are we really okay with a vision of God that makes him look like an ISIS terrorist who burns his enemies alive?

Isn't this image of God just making us afraid of him?

And if it is, is this the right image?

One of the good things that I hope will come about through the existence of ISIS is people realizing that if their theology makes God look like a terrorist setting fire to his enemies and watching them smolder with glee, then their theology is hopelessly screwed up and needs to be completely discarded. And that includes you. There is no love in terror, and there is no terror in love. These things *are* mutually exclusive and cannot coexist together. Either love wins, or fear wins.

God is not like an ISIS terrorist; God is *love*.

God is not to be feared, but far too many of us haven't been told that yet.

I'm someone who didn't receive that message until a little later in life, and all the years I spent fearing God finally caught up with me one day.

The Midlife Crisis

They say that going through a midlife crisis isn't so uncommon, but I don't suppose that makes it any easier to go through one—especially when that midlife crisis is rooted in a crisis of faith on top of all the other things about life we reconsider when we hit middle age.

When it hit me, I felt like I had been run over by a truck. I mean, it *really* sucked.

It was like I woke up one day and realized I was supposed to have arrived somewhere by now but instead had this acute realization that I hadn't arrived anywhere at all. And if I had "arrived," then wow—"arriving" felt a lot different from what I had imagined or hoped for.

I felt lost. I had turned forty years old and was still waiting to become a homeowner; I was driving a car with 230,000 miles on it that I was sure would shit the bed any day (update: it did while I was writing the later chapters of this book); I was trying to cope and deal with the grief of adopting four children but only getting to raise one of them;[2] my marriage was crumbling before my eyes; and on top of all that, I felt like my faith was dying. Or maybe it was dead—I wasn't always sure.

My faith crisis was the last straw that sent me into a long spiral that I didn't know I would ever pull out of. All the other things were potentially survivable, but the faith part is what I thought would kill me—*because my faith had always been something that sustained me through the painful seasons of life.* I had lost my church, my pastorate, and all my friends over a few crazy Jesus-y ideas (hating guns and loving gays will do it every time). It was almost unbearable for me to even consider a loss of faith as a possibility on top of all these changes to my Christian community, my personal losses, and potential losses. Yet, I could only deny reality for so long: I wasn't sure what I believed anymore, or even *if* I believed anymore.

God had never felt farther away from me, and I had never felt so afraid.

To complicate things, even though I had found myself in this dark place where I was unsure about everything other than the fact that my faith didn't work for me anymore, I outwardly appeared both successful and a little bit lucky. I had started a blog about my spiritual transition out of fundamentalist Christianity that became quite popular almost overnight; I had begun getting book deal offers without even seeking them out; I had found myself traveling and speaking around the world, getting invites to talk shows and national radio programs; and I quickly had become seen as a "Christian influencer," with millions of people reading my work each year. So traversing a spiritual midlife crisis seemed even more complicated, because I felt like scores of people were watching my journey and expecting me to be a person who provided them with answers to the hard questions. I was supposed to be the one *helping* those with a crisis of faith; I was not supposed to be the one who *needed* the help.

"What would they think if they knew what I am going through?" I wondered.

Being a public figure within Christianity had a suffocating effect on my personal process, as I felt like my faith and life were under a microscope. I had become known for helping people deconstruct their faith, inviting them to follow along with me. My hope all along had been to lead people to somewhere better, to some *thing* better, than what so many of us grew up with. But where I was landing? I wasn't in a better place at all, and I didn't want to be responsible for bringing other people there with me.

What if all the work I had done was actually leading people— and leading myself—to a total collapse of faith? Total confusion? What if the critics were right and I was leading people in the *wrong* direction? My intent had never been for people to lose their faith; in fact, I wanted to be someone who helped people find faith after they *thought* they had lost it. I wanted to help them reclaim it, revive it, and thrive within it.

But that's not where I found myself; I was far, far away from the place I had desired to be. It was as if I had woken up one morning and become the very person I had always longed to help. But in that dark space, I couldn't even help myself.

I. Was. Stuck.

With each new day, I had started to worry that all of my deconstruction had backfired on me, because it *felt* like everything I had believed was no longer true—and I didn't know where I was supposed to begin my journey to wherever I needed to go next.

All I knew was that I was so scared I could hardly move—because *every direction felt like the wrong direction.*

When You're Stuck in Scared

For a while I had a sneaking suspicion that my midlife crisis was rooted in a crisis of faith, but it took me a while to fully connect the dots and realize that it wasn't just a general faith crisis, but the natural outcome of trying to live out a fear-based faith. It took God bringing a few people into my life to help illuminate this for me, but once they appeared, it was a case of not being able to un-see what was now clearly visible to me.

I still remember the day I was sitting in my counselor Joel's office when I finally got to the root of it all. "Who the hell taught you that you're not going to be okay?" Joel asked me. "You've told me military stories about having to hop off a plane and run like hell because you guys weren't sure if there were snipers in the area; you've survived your way through all sorts of insurmountable life challenges over the years, and yet somehow you're sitting here in front of me with a doctorate, *and* you're covered in tattoos that look like they *had* to be painful."

Leaning slightly forward, he continued: "So when you tell me how afraid you are, it feels like when a beautiful woman tells you she thinks she's ugly. It seems silly to *everyone but her.* I look at you and think that *you're the only person in the world who doesn't believe you're going to be okay.* I'm convinced it's because somewhere in your childhood you were given the message that you're unable to navigate hard times without life falling apart—but no matter how many times you do this successfully, you keep believing the old childhood tapes in your head. It's as if somewhere, somehow, you got stuck in scared."

I had a love-hate relationship with Joel. I loved him because he was unlike any counselor I had ever had, and I hated him because he was unlike any counselor I had ever had. He didn't quietly nod and rubber-stamp everything I said, and he didn't let me blame others for my choices and experiences in life; he always brought everything back to me. Joel argued that just about everything could be traced back to childhood[3]—and he didn't let me off the hook when it was time to go there. He'd poke and prod, and some sessions he'd sit there and ask me the same question over and over until I really wrestled with the answer—and found it.

For me, every issue we processed seemed to keep coming back to the same root. No matter what was going on in my life, or what problem I was trying to work my way through, within ten minutes into the discussion we'd begin to pull the layers of the onion back and see what was really going on: I was afraid. We discovered that I was afraid of just about everything but had never realized it. Somehow, after all of my theological deconstruction, I was still living a life that was rooted in paralyzing fear. And it was precisely my fear—not anything else—that had power to make everything unravel if I didn't confront it head-on.

They say that when fear is triggered, people move into either "fight" mode or "flight" mode—they either attack the source of their fear, or they run from it. My issue with fear, however, had taken me to a different place: I was completely frozen.[4] It had gotten so intense for me that I'd show up for every session with Joel, sit down on the couch, and say the same thing: "I feel stuck and don't know what to do." We would almost laugh about it because we both knew what I was going to say when I walked in, sat down, and opened my mouth.

I've heard stories of rock climbers who made it halfway up the side of a sheer cliff and got stuck—not because they were actually stuck, but because they panicked. In these situations the panic can be so incapacitating that they lose not only the ability to keep climbing upward but also the ability to climb down. Fear can freeze us in place. Sometimes in life we can deal with fear preemptively, sometimes we can deal with it in the moment, and sometimes fear has a way of bringing life to a screeching halt until we're unable to focus on anything beyond the fear itself.

For me? Well, I was at one of those screeching halt moments. Like it or not, I wasn't going anywhere until I faced fear—and had a paradigm shift that would invite me to either keep climbing up into the unknown, or at the very least, to climb back down to the safety of what I used to know.

For people frozen with fear in a rock climbing situation, I'm told the best thing they can do is stop, breathe, and think through their fears until they're able to compose themselves and move again. Being frozen with fear feels like forever, but you can't stay there— eventually you have to choose up or down and start moving in that direction. Because if you stay stuck in scared, you can die; but if you confront it and push past it, you have the possibility of a new day to explore a wide-open life.

Although my fear seemed to have generalized into nearly every facet of my middle-aged life, I knew there had to be a genesis to it all—and I think Joel knew that, too. He would invite me to go back and then further back in my story, often saying: "You're dancing for someone. You're trying to keep someone happy. You're really afraid of pissing someone off if you live a life that's different from the miserable life you're living. Who is it? Who are you trying to impress or appease? Is it your mom? Is it your dad? Is it . . . ?"

And one day, it hit me: this was all about *God*. At least, this all had its root in God.

I was reminded of the ISIS video and the images of the Jordanian pilot dying in the flames, and I realized that *that* was exactly what I thought God was going to do to me if I screwed something up, got something wrong, or didn't love him back in the right way. When I was a child, this fear motivated me to constantly govern my behavior, but as a middle-aged adult with a keen awareness that each birthday represented a year closer to death, and what came after death, that fear paralyzed me.

And that's when it finally came together in my mind: we can hold a fear-based foundational understanding of God or a love-based understanding of God, but we cannot hold both. Love doesn't fear, and fear can't love.

In my case, however, I was still scared of him. (Or her. Or whatever the proper pronoun is for a genderless God.) I had already deconstructed so much of my fundamentalist/conservative evangelical faith, but the issue of fear became for me one of those situations of being able to take the boy out of the town, but not the town out of the boy. It was my blind spot—the one I completely overlooked, as I was outwardly expressing a belief in a faith that was already beyond the fear. The truth, as I had come to discover it, was that I was still living out a fear-based faith regardless of what I claimed. I think our experience of Christianity, and religion in general, is usually rooted in fear because religions are designed to address the one fear we all hold in common, whether we admit it or not: death. When the God we believe in has a list of dos and don'ts and one misstep can land us in torment for eternity— something worse than death—it's no wonder that we might end up living a fear-based faith, whether we're conservative, liberal, or something in between.

My faith journey had expressions across the liberal-to-conservative spectrum, but fear followed me wherever I went because I still believed in a God who was constantly grading me and looking for a reason to deny me life after death. When I was a conservative Christian, the God I believed in was grading me on the basis of what I did with my penis, whether or not I smoked or drank, and how firmly I stood against abortion. When I became a progressive Christian, I functionally believed in the same God, but he was grading me on different things. Instead of genital usage, he graded me on what I did with my money, how I used my privilege, and how courageously I spoke up for the poor and marginalized. These were completely different expressions of the same faith, but they had one thing in common: belief in a God who was incessantly policing me in order to determine whether I deserved life or eternal torment. The same God of Fear ruled both religions.

Liberal versus conservative aside, I couldn't live like that anymore. Like harvesting termite-riddled lumber to use as the frame for a new house, my entire spiritual journey was doomed unless I gutted and destroyed the very thing my faith had been built upon. In fact, if I wanted to survive—minimally, in a spiritual sense—there wasn't any other choice.

This was the foundation of my fear-based faith—the foundation I could never shake even when I didn't think I believed most of it anymore. For all the unintended consequences of some expressions of the Christian religion, I think fear is the most devastating—because fear has a way of permeating all areas of our lives. Like a cancer that can spread far beyond the point of origin, fear has the ability to spread from limb to limb until organ failure and death happen in parts of our bodies that had nothing to do with the root of it all. Fear is the ultimate causation of bystander casualties, and a faith rooted in the fear of God will bring death to places inside us that we didn't even know could die.

I had climbed halfway up the mountain, but my foundation of fear—rooted in a fear of God—had caused my faith and the rest of life to come to a screeching halt. I reached a place where I was too afraid to make any decisions, because I didn't want to make the wrong one. Spending so many years being afraid I'd someday be tormented in hell led me to becoming radically indecisive, because I felt like making no decision was better than making the wrong one. If the smallest sin, theological technicality, or error can land us in hell, it's reasonable that we reach a point of being so afraid that we try to become Switzerland[5] and remain neutral on critical issues and decisions—not just in faith, but in everyday life.

That was me. I was afraid to be honest with myself about what I did or did not believe anymore. I was afraid to make decisions for my life that would lead to greater happiness because I was afraid I'd get it wrong and end up on the wrong end of God's wrath. I was as stuck in scared as anyone on the planet has ever been, and truth be told, that became a safe place—because being stuck and indecisive about life gives us the permission to refuse to take any risks beyond the risk of doing *nothing*.

For those of us who get stuck in fear, we reach a point where indecision is no longer a plausible option if we want to truly live. The months and years of running from fear and abdicating our full engagement with faith and life have a way of catching up to us. Eventually, the walls close in. The trail ends. The sun dips below the horizon. We reach a point where we either have to close our eyes and spend the rest of our lives pretending we're not dying, or we need to embrace a bold authenticity about who we are and what we believe. We need to embrace life itself. I was at such a crossroads, but I was still stuck. I needed a mental reframe, a boost—I needed *something* to nudge me in whatever direction I was supposed to go. I needed to be unafraid.

My "Aha!" Moment

The most important moments in life are those small flashes that happen when something shifts in our thought processes, and we begin to see things differently. I cherish these reframing moments, because even though they may seem quick or insignificant, they actually change *everything*. They are the domino that tips all the others.

The "aha!" moment that allowed me to begin the process of getting unstuck from fear came one day while I was having a conversation with Rob Bell on my podcast "That God Show."[6] I asked him, "What would you say to someone who doesn't know what he or she believes anymore?"—not realizing I was actually asking a question about my own faith crisis.

Rob essentially rejected the premise of my question and said that it's not accurate that a person doesn't know what he or she believes anymore; instead, he said, "In that moment they are just acutely aware of some things that they *don't* believe anymore."

Rob's response was the first piece of advice that helped me regain my bearings from where I was frozen midway up the mountain. In that moment I felt like I was still knee-deep in my spiritual midlife crisis, frozen with fear and unsure what I believed or even if I believed anymore; but as I listened to his answer, I quickly realized that maybe I was exactly where I needed to be. I just needed a mental reframe to help me see where I needed to climb from that stuck place. Thus, his answer wasn't some sort of road map; it was more like a decoder ring

that helped me look back at my spiritual journey and finally
make sense of where I had been and where I found myself in the
present moment on the mountain.

Rob was right. It was not true that I *did not know* what I believed
anymore; instead, I secretly knew inside that I no longer believed
in being afraid—especially of God. In this case, knowing what I
did not believe became the key to rediscovering what I *did believe*.
Sure, I felt stuck on the side of the mountain, but maybe it was
because in that moment I needed to look down—to look back—and
to look good and hard at where I had come from, and to rethink all
of it from a standpoint of being . . . unafraid.

For those of us who have experienced a faith shift or
deconstruction of our faith, it's entirely normal to come to a
point in our journey where we feel afraid. It's also completely
normal, when that fear is left unchecked, for it to spread
throughout all aspects of our faith and life until we lose sight
of where we're even headed. We get stuck in scared and forget
that we have to stay there only if we choose to stay there.
Writing now from the other end of the journey, I can say that
it's a far better option to recognize when we're stuck in scared
and to insist on moving *somewhere*.

Yes, to become hyperaware of the things we don't believe
anymore can be scary; we become afraid of being wrong, afraid of
becoming social outcasts within our faith circles, afraid of what
God will do to us for getting some parts of life incorrect. And more
than anything, I think we become afraid that naming those things
we don't believe anymore will result in a *loss of faith instead of
the birth of it*. But in fact, I have come to believe that making the
conscious decision to be unafraid and name those things we don't
believe anymore can lead us to explore a faith that is wide-open
and beautiful beyond our wildest imagination.

Moving Beyond Fear-Based Faith

From meeting and talking to people across the country, I've become well aware that there's nothing new or unique about having a crisis of faith. My story, in many ways, is the same story I've heard repeated over and over in many different conversations. While our stories all have their individual flavors, I believe that we all share common roots in fear—and that's precisely why I decided to write this book.

Yes, I was going through a crisis of faith—teetering between feeling like I didn't know what I believed anymore, and moments when I was acutely aware of some things I no longer believed but for a time was too afraid to acknowledge and to explore deeper.

Thankfully, I decided to lean into it to see what I could learn from the journey.

The intensity of a crisis of faith feels like the world is crashing down on us, especially if we grew up believing that having strong, secure, and confident faith is one of the most important foundations in life. However, what I've come to learn on this journey is this: a crisis of faith might not be a crisis at all.

I mean, what if it were possible to shed old beliefs and not be left empty-handed?

What if confronting the things we *don't* believe is exactly how we discover what we *do* believe?

What if a faith crisis is actually something God has orchestrated in order to free us from false beliefs about him, false beliefs about ourselves, and false beliefs about others?

What if deciding to be unafraid and to lean into those intense moments of a faith crisis in fact leads us to the birth of faith instead of the death of it?

And what if this is exactly what God wants us to do, and is inviting us to do?

I believe all of these "what-ifs" are true, because that is exactly what I discovered on my journey to embrace a crisis of faith as a divine opportunity. On the pages that follow I'm going to invite you to lean into the tension, to confront some fears, and to discover the vibrant new life that awaits you and all the dominoes that can fall if you simply decide to be unafraid.

Having the Courage to Step Out

Realizing that I no longer believed it was good, helpful, or wise to be afraid of God anymore may sound like a single issue—but it's not. A. W. Tozer once said that "what comes into our minds when we think about God is the most important thing about us," and I have found this to be true. What we think about God completely shapes and filters how we view every aspect of our faith and life, even if we aren't able to consciously connect all the dots. Making the conscious decision to reject a fear-based God is the floodgate that leads us to experience not the loss of faith but freedom from fear-based faith in order to discover a truer and deeper faith. It is the one step that will immediately, and often shockingly, thrust us into a whole new world of faith that we didn't even know existed. Saying goodbye to the fear-based God and his fear-based faith is a catapult, not a brick wall. What's more, we will soon discover that it is God who is inviting us to embark on this journey.

The process goes something like this: If I don't believe in being afraid of God anymore, what does that mean I *do* believe about God? Having the courage to be unafraid and say "I don't believe *this*" will almost always lead us to be able to stand up and say "which means, I do believe *this*."

Yup. It's scary to name for the first time what we don't believe—but *wow*, it's beyond amazing to be able to step forward and then name what we actually *do* believe once we move beyond the fear to the wide-open life of being unafraid.

I think we often avoid and delay this necessary process because of the order of events—naming what we don't believe in order to discover what we do believe. The fear of what we don't know can often be more powerful than what we currently do know. As a result, we miss out on what is life-giving and fulfilling because we're more content to opt for the stale comfort of what feels predictable to us. But let me warn you: "predictable" has the power to kill. In order to step out into faith and find freedom and new life, we have to become more willing to experience the sensation of the unknown rather than stick with a status quo that's killing us. This is a process we must actively choose—no one can do it for us. But you'll find that there are plenty of people willing to join you once you're out there.

Although this is a process, it is a process that begins with one big leap—and trust me, that first leap is the hardest part. But once you take it, some of the fears you currently have will subside, and you'll be introduced to a host of new thoughts and feelings—and many of them will feel surprisingly good. However, it's that big first step that currently stands in the way—because let's be honest: to say "I'm not afraid of God anymore" is a pretty giant leap for any of us who grew up in a conservative flavor of Christianity.

When I think about my own spiritual journey and what it was like to finally acknowledge that it was time for me to step out into uncharted faith, shed some beliefs, and begin actively searching for new ones, I'm taken back to a similar moment in life—one where I was standing in a plane two miles above the Philippine Sea, realizing that once I stepped out of that plane, there was no turning back. I had always wanted to go skydiving, but I had no idea how terrifying it would be to stand at the plane's door and feel and hear the rush of wind blowing about my face. If I had been left to my own devices, I most likely would have marched myself back to my seat and sat down; but since I was strapped to the master diver, I didn't have much choice. He ended up jumping for both of us.

Although a host of fears led up to that moment, most of them were fears of the unknown. However, here's the funny thing about fearing the unknown: these fears tend to quickly dissipate once we step *toward* the unknown. I firmly believe that these types of fears can exist and thrive only as long as we're *standing still*. The minute we take a step forward, followed by another step forward, they recede. In my experience, those types of fears can't survive as long as we're doing that; they exist right until the moment we confront them.

My fear around skydiving lasted for about three seconds after I jumped from the plane. But then, in the twinkling of an eye, that fear was replaced by tremendous feelings of awe and excitement. As I watched the ground rush up at me at terminal velocity and explored what it felt like to feel totally weightless, I was overcome with gratitude that I hadn't let that fear of the first step keep me from embracing the full experience I was now having. From inside the plane—what I knew and was comfortable with—the world outside of the plane seemed terrifying. But I discovered that stepping into the unknown (the very thing I had feared) turned out to be one of the most exhilarating experiences of my life and opened my eyes to a new way of seeing the world around me. (I mean, come on—how could you not see the world differently after watching the ground rush up at you, knowing that the only thing between you and certain death was some string and nylon in a backpack that *someone else* was wearing?)

For many of us practicing Americanized Christianity, we grew up being fed a list of things that "true Christians" believe—and I'm convinced that all those things were rooted in a fear of God. You memorize the script, do what you're told, stop asking questions, and life is fine . . . for a time. As with any faith structure or worldview, toxic stuff has a way of slipping past the goalie from time to time, making the process of letting some beliefs go up in flames absolutely necessary for a healthy, vibrant faith. In fact, if you sift through the ashes of faith purposefully, you'll find something far more beautiful and life-giving than what you started out with in the first place.

Discovering What Sculptors Have Known All Along

Reclaiming a vibrant faith by way of removing elements of our faith is frightening and *seems* counterintuitive—but I assure you, it's not. For those of us who have histories of wrestling with our faith, and spiritual and religious baggage, we may still be haunted by hurtful experiences and misconceptions about who God is, and who we are; and there comes a time when learning and healing can occur only when we embrace a process of unlearning some of the damaging and life-choking lies we have believed, and then replace them with something better. In fact, I believe *even Jesus himself taught this.*

Jesus once told his disciples that if anyone wanted to follow him, they had to first become like little children again. Various scholars and Bible teachers may interpret this differently, but I believe Jesus was referring to the necessity of unlearning all those broken ways of thinking that drain the life and faith from us. It's as if Jesus is inviting us to take everything we've ever believed, dismantle it, and start over with something better.

Consider for a moment what we as adults have that children do not have. Children do not have (we hope) the amount of emotional and spiritual baggage that we adults tend to carry around. Young children do not have decades of indoctrination to undo. They do not have years of lingering pain from experiencing church splits or being betrayed by a spouse. Children have not had to sit with twenty-five years of being convinced that God hates them and is angry with them. Children have not (yet) had the time to so deeply internalize the negative messages we are taught about God and ourselves, that their self-image becomes almost hopelessly broken.

Instead, children are a clean slate—they are eager to learn and soak everything up. True, they will end up learning either affirming messages or destructive ones, but they don't begin that way. Children are not preprogrammed; they can be molded and shaped. When Jesus said that we must come to him as little children, I believe he was speaking to the fact that to truly understand who God is, and who we are as a result, we need to name those things that are no longer true and then begin asking what actually *is* true. I believe this process invites us to trust what sculptors have always known: there's something beautiful to be revealed underneath the mess of it all.

When sculptors begin creating, they begin with a giant block of stone and a handful of tools. But instead of building each piece individually of whatever they are creating, sculptors create *by means of subtraction*. They do not add *to* the lump, and they do not immediately begin forming the lump; instead, they remove the unnecessary parts of it *first*. With each layer they skillfully shave off, what lies beneath eventually begins to be revealed. It can be difficult to see this at first, especially if an observer does not have a precise visual of what the sculptor is intending. Instead, the observer must simply watch the outer layers be removed and discarded and trust that the sculptor has something beautiful in mind that he or she wishes to reveal when the process of subtraction is completed. Once all of the unnecessary or useless parts of the stone are removed, the sculptor can then shape what is left until it looks exactly the way he or she intends.

Just like a giant block of unformed stone, faith can be messy and confusing. Yet, with skillful hands, we can sort trash from treasure and turn that messy lump into something we had no idea existed underneath all the clutter.

This is a book about moving beyond a fear-based faith, which is possible only once we move beyond a fear-based God. It's also a book about all the amazing things we can discover once we remove fear from the heart of our faith. It's a book about no longer being afraid to confront or ignore the dead aspects of faith—things that are untrue, destructive, or divisive—and confronting those things in a way that can lead us to somewhere better instead of leaving us empty-handed the way some forms of deconstruction left many of us.

Most of all, this is a book about confronting our fear-based faith and then "un-ing" it—turning afraid into *un*afraid—so we can get closer to God.

Let me be direct: the Bible says that God did not give us a spirit of *fear,* but one of *power and love.*[7] If this is true, which I believe it is, it means that fear-based faith is not of God. It's not from God, it doesn't please God, and it's not what God wants.

Thus, a process of shedding fear-based faith isn't simply what's wise and healthy—it actually honors God, and honors his desire that we not have a spirit of fear.

Now, a few words about me. This isn't a book written by someone who had a unique and isolated experience. I'm not the guy who got his arm trapped between two rocks while hiking and then used a dull pocket knife to cut his arm off so he could flee to safety. I didn't experience a shipwreck and spend forty days lost at sea where I survived by catching fish with my hands and drinking my own urine. I didn't get kidnapped by ISIS and live to tell a harrowing tale of befriending my captors and escaping under the cover of darkness with the help of a kind goat farmer (although, I *did* actually get abducted once in the Congo, and once is enough for me).

Instead, I'm just an ordinary guy who grew up learning some really negative and damaging messages about who God is, and who I was as a result. I'm just a Christian who spent much of his life stuck in scared but who realized that this scared place was all deeply connected to my understanding of God. For most of my life, I didn't question these views about God and about myself, leading me to a moment when everything I believed came crumbling down—almost taking me with it.

But I suppose if there is something unique about me, if there is something different about my spiritual journey that might teach you something, it is this: I woke up one morning and decided that I wanted to know what my life and faith might look like if I chose to be unafraid; so I took a good, hard look at my fear and decided to "un" it, so that I could in turn help you do the same.

2.

THE GOD I JUST COULDN'T BELIEVE IN ANYMORE

Where do we even begin identifying and discarding the aspects of our faith that are choking the life out of us so we can start the search for something better? For those who want to move beyond a fear-based faith and explore the wide-open life that we just *have* to believe exists over the horizon, what's the first step?

For me, in order to move past my fear-based faith, I needed to move past my fear-based God. Surely, if God is the supreme being of the universe, if God is the central focus of faith, then naming what we don't believe about this God anymore might be the place to start on this new faith journey. For me, it was slightly more specific—yes, I knew I needed to begin with God, but what I really needed to begin with was that one thing that seemed to drive my spiritual life, from the moment I first became a believer until the present day: hair-raising fear.

We Americans sure do love us some fear—it's why preachers peddle it, why politicians thrive on it, and how Stephen King got rich off of it. Fear is why we've spent years as a nation at preemptive war, it is how Donald Trump became the president of the United States, and it is the face behind a thousand masks. Fear is deeply ingrained in the American psyche and has a way of permeating all the many crevices of culture—including our faith. And it is here where fear becomes the most destructive foundational force anyone could build upon.

I didn't come to completely appreciate the overwhelming power of fear in a relationship until I began what I came to call "therapeutic parenting." A few years back, my wife and I had decided that instead of producing biological children, one of our callings in life was to adopt older children in need of families. Statistics show that although adoption is a popular trend in evangelical circles, older children who have been institutionalized tend to be adopted into loving families far less often than younger children. Once we came to see the need for families to adopt these older children, we knew that we wanted to be one of them—and so, in 2011 we became the proud parents to two girls from Peru, ages eight and twelve.

On one hand, I'd like to say that we didn't go into this with our heads in the clouds or with unreasonable expectations of what parenting would be like. We knew that adopting older children would bring a unique set of challenges; we tried to familiarize ourselves with what those challenges might be and how we might respond to them when the time came. In hindsight, I think that we prepared as best as we could, but the reality is that some things are simply unknown ahead of time—and it is hard to prepare for something if you don't know how you should be preparing for it.

As I look back on the years between the adoption and today, I see areas of parenting where we were totally prepared and areas where we faced unexpected challenges—areas where there was little we could have done to be prepared for reality. One of those unexpected challenges came by way of trauma triggers; our children had past traumatic experiences that would become unintentionally triggered from time to time. These triggers could often come without warning, and when they did, life would quickly get interesting. Sure, maybe you have an exploding diaper story that happened in the middle of the supermarket, but adoptive parents of older children often have their own supermarket stories that are equally as colorful and messy.

Through the years I've learned a lot from parenting children with traumatic histories, but perhaps the biggest of those lessons is just how overwhelming fear can be. I saw it in myself, and I saw it in my children. Intellectually, I realized the power of fear from my own personal experiences of being afraid, but seeing fear from a different angle—seeing fear manifest in my own children—has completely changed my view of it and brought me to the understanding of how life-killing fear can be. This is particularly true with how I saw fear manifest in one of my children, who seemed to have fear triggers every night.

In the early stages of our adoption story, one of my daughters faced triggers and fears that I'm not sure she was even able to verbalize. Shortly after we all settled in at home back in the United States, it became clear that she had a powerful fear of reabandonment. This fear would appear night after night in the form of her waking up and wandering into our bedroom to stare quietly at us as we slept. Predictably, just as we had fallen asleep, we'd be woken by the pitter-patter of little feet coming into our room and would see a silhouette standing at the edge of our bed. Sometimes she would let me walk her back to bed, but other times she was paralyzed with fear—becoming almost catatonic as she stood trembling by our bed.

Those moments when our daughter was full of fear became the

most emotionally painful moments of parenting. Whether it was during one of her midnight checks to make sure her mom and I hadn't left her, or other situations where she froze with fear, I felt completely helpless and unable to reach her when the fear took over. Each time I would rush to her and try to cradle her in my arms and let her know she was safe and loved, but my attempts were often rebuffed; many nights she would not let me get near her. It was as if the child I knew and loved—the child so full of life and vitality—would temporarily disappear and a completely different child would take over. In those moments it was still true that she had a dad who loved her more than anything in the world, but the presence of fear made her *totally incapable of receiving or experiencing love.* While I'm sure those moments of being so afraid that she became incapable of receiving love were horrible for her, they were also tremendously painful for me because *all I wanted to do was give her love.*

At the same time, my other daughter struggled with fear as well, but in very different ways. Whereas one loved being in a family so much that she was afraid we'd leave her in the night, the other had a trauma related to conditions that ended up making the love of a family *really, really scary.* For her, whenever she'd begin to feel the love and intimacy of being in a family, fear would rise to the surface and manifest itself in ways that likewise prevented her from feeling and experiencing love. For both children, fear became a wall that—at least for a season—kept love *out.* This experience drove home for me the reality of what the Bible teaches when it says "God did not give us the spirit of fear." I didn't fully realize the depths of that until I ran to my own children with love, only to discover that they were too afraid to receive it.

No, fear does not come from God—because God is love, and fear is love's enemy.

Fear and love are perhaps the two most powerful feelings in the human experience, but it is important to realize that fear is the enemy of love. Love and fear are not harmonious dance partners but two warring sides that each long to eradicate the other. Fear makes it impossible to experience love, but as the Bible reminds us, perfect love throws fear out of the picture. We may find fear and love mixed together, but when we do, what we are really seeing is a fight to the death where only one side will win. Love eventually wins, or fear does—but it's always one or the other.

When love and fear are mixed together, it is a death match. Always.

Let's pause for a second, because I want this to sink in: when the Bible describes the opposite of love, *it doesn't describe hate*. The Bible says that the opposite of love is actually *fear*—meaning that where there is love, there cannot be fear. They are adversaries.

I've often said that I've learned more about God from adopting children with special needs than I did from eight years of seminary training, and that couldn't be more true than when it comes to the issue of fear. As I experienced the many ways in which fear made the full experience of a parent's love so difficult, I began to see that fear is not something that can be foundationally present in a relationship. Fear is something that kills relationships and closes the door to love. *Fear is a relationship killer, not a relationship builder.*

This realization led me to a new question: If fear is the opposite of love, and if fear is toxic to relationships, why do we so often make fear foundational to our relationship with God? If we wouldn't spray the soil of our gardens with a toxic chemical that kills plants instead of making them grow, why would we saturate our faith with the one thing that makes for a nonstarter in our spiritual lives?

Maybe you've realized this before, or maybe you're just awakening to it, but I believe that far too many of us are raised on a version of Christianity that is built on a foundation of fear and that this false foundation is a threat to our entire belief system. I know for certain that my faith was predicated on the foundation of fear, and as I began to wrestle with how to best give my spiritual life CPR, I realized that if we don't address the issue of fear, we will never have a vibrant faith that is defined by an abundance of freedom-giving love.

You Can't Build a Relationship on a Foundation of Fear

The first 832 times I asked Jesus into my heart, I did so out of complete fear. It was the same paralyzing, chest-gripping fear that I saw overcome my daughters, and it was a fear that in many ways dominated much of my childhood. I was taught many things about God, but the one thing that stuck with me was the threat of being tortured and burned alive for all of eternity if I didn't ask Jesus into my heart. As we say here in New England, *I was scared shitless*.

There's a meme that circles the Internet from time to time that always reminds me of my earlier understanding of God. It's the classic picture of Jesus standing at the door and knocking. The voice behind the door asks, "Who's there?"

"It's me, Jesus. Let me in."

"Why should I let you in?" the voice replies.

"So I can save you," Jesus says.

"Save me from what?" the voice asks.

The meme ends with Jesus responding, *"From what I'm going to do to you if you don't let me in!"*

While the version of my childhood was slightly different—God was the dual personality who both loved me unconditionally but also was more than willing to torture me, and Jesus was the good guy who offered to protect me from his angry dad—the result was the same: the foundation of my faith was fear. And this was how I came to be the kid who habitually asked Jesus into his heart, and the adult who nightly prayed that God would forgive me of any sin I had forgotten to confess. I was convinced that my eternal fate could be screwed up on a technicality.

"What if I haven't really asked Jesus into my heart, and I'm just remembering incorrectly?" I'd wonder.

"What if even the smallest unconfessed sin lands me in hell forever? Am I forgetting to mention one and dooming myself to an eternity of torture?"

I was haunted by these fears, day and night.

I'd like to say that I've completely moved past this, but some days the one known as the Formerly Fundie still is haunted by those thoughts. Old habits die hard.

Perhaps what is more disturbing is that my foundation of fear was no accident. I didn't misunderstand what I was taught. I didn't get things twisted in my undeveloped mind, I wasn't confused, and I certainly didn't misinterpret anything. The version of Christianity I grew up with was predicated on fear—and in many ways, dominant forms of Christianity in the United States still are.

You see, like many of us, I grew up with an understanding of God that was less than warm and fuzzy. As an adult I realized that as a child, I was introduced to God in conjunction with being introduced to hell. For most of my childhood the only thing I feared more than hell was getting left behind in the rapture and

having to endure the long seven-year tribulation before either
being beheaded or getting sent to hell (more on that later). And yes,
then there was Jesus—the person who always fascinated me and
made me feel loved—but even Jesus sounded great in large part
because God was so fear-worthy: Jesus was the only one who could
protect you from what his angry dad wanted to do to you—and
what he wanted to do to you was the most horrific thing you could
ever imagine. The suggestion that this sort of foundation to faith
could lead to some really bad consequences shouldn't be shocking
to anyone.

Many modern American Christian preachers and figures make
no apology for or attempt to hide the fact that they are selling a
religion founded upon fear. I once heard a prominent evangelist
say that one of the biggest barriers to evangelization is that we
don't do a good enough job of instilling fear in people. To him, the
church is full of "false converts" (what we used to call "backsliders"
growing up) because they aren't afraid enough of hell—a problem
the rest of us are supposed to rectify by helping them become
really, really afraid of God. Others, particularly leaders in the
Calvinist movement, make a similar case by arguing that it's not
possible to experience God's love until we are sufficiently afraid of
what he's going to do to us if we don't love him back in the right
way. Sadly, too many Christian leaders see fear of God as a cure,
without realizing it is actually *the poison*. They see fear and love
not as enemies at war with one another but as some strangely
compatible dance partners beautifully waltzing in harmony
together.

But that's not how fear and love work.

I have often wondered whether such leaders truly believe
what they're selling and whether they think the concept of fear
being a precursor to the experience of love would translate

into human relationships. What if, on the day I first met my daughters at the orphanage, I said to them, "I love you, but if you don't love me back the way I want, and if you don't perfectly follow every instruction I give to you, I'm going to torture you forever"?

Do those Christian leaders seriously believe that a healthy relationship can begin on such a foundation? Is it possible to truly love someone who uses the threat of torture to force a relationship? At best, such threats might earn a terrified compliance, but they can never earn love—and call me crazy, *but I think God is aiming at love.*

When we translate the concept of fear into human relationships, we see that it's not just absurd, but *totally obscene.* How can something be understood as sick, twisted, and abusive when we do it but good, perfect, and right when God does it? How would you feel if your son or daughter introduced you to the person he or she had picked to be a lifelong mate and that person told you, "I really love your child, but because my love is so perfect, and my ways are higher than your ways, I'm going to have to set them on fire if they get out of line"? You'd tell that a person to get the hell away from your family.

Fear of God doesn't draw us closer to God; it drives us farther away—and any time something drives us away from God, that should be a strong sign that such a thing has *no place* in the Christian faith.

We run away from things we are afraid of—we never run toward them.

And this, I believe, is the foundation of what is preventing so many people from experiencing the beauty of who God really is: most expressions of Christianity are built upon a foundation of fear, and *that foundation dooms the entire building.*

God Is Not an ISIS Terrorist

An old Christian bumper sticker popular with the hellfire folks reads, "Christianity isn't a religion, it's a relationship." While I would argue it's a religion based on a relationship, this brings me to another question: Could you really and truly have a loving relationship with an ISIS terrorist who burns people alive? Could you really love that person? Feel safe with that person? Feel comfortable sharing the depths of your soul with that person? If an ISIS terrorist was your friend or lover, wouldn't you always have a nagging fear in the back of your mind that one day that person might turn on you for some displeasing offense, however unintentional that offense may have been?

A healthy and loving relationship cannot begin with fear. Quite the contrary, a healthy and loving relationship actually dispels fear. Thinking back to my daughters, I see that fear existed in our relationship, but only because fear came with them to the relationship. Instead of affirming those fears, I have spent years loving them as best as I can, with the goal of *loving the fear right out of them completely.*

If God is the perfect father, and I—a completely flawed father—am busy loving the fear out of my children, doesn't it make sense that God is probably busy doing the same thing for us? And what if God is actually a lot better at loving than we are?

What if God isn't someone we should be afraid of, but instead is the one being who can perfectly love the fear right out of us?

Some preachers will say that fear of God is good and healthy, that fear at times can help us avoid danger and undesired consequences—and this last part is actually true. These preachers point out, for instance, that fear of snakes can help you avoid getting bitten and perhaps killed. A fear of heights can help prevent you from falling off a cliff and being obliterated upon landing. A fear of alligators, hippos, and all other sorts of beasts of the field may keep you alert enough to avoid being ripped to shreds. And yes, they are partially correct—fear in such cases can be helpful and wise. Fear is not useless.

But here's the problem: God is not a rattlesnake that is waiting to inject deadly venom into you if you stray past it in the wrong way. God is not a cliff that you might fall over. God is not a territorial hippo that will chase you down and gore you if you're in the wrong place at the wrong time. God is not an alligator that will rip your arm off. And God sure as hell is not an ISIS terrorist displaying a total depravity and lack of love and mercy as he douses someone with petrol and lights that person on fire.

God is not any of those things, nor like any of those things, and to compare God—the ultimate expression of love—to such things is nothing short of a satanic distortion of the ultimate reality.

A foundation built upon being afraid makes any sort of meaningful relationship impossible. Sure, you could have a relationship similar to that of master and fearful servant, but not a relationship of mutual friendship—and one of the last things Jesus reminded his disciples was that he would no longer call them servants, but instead, they were now friends.[1]

When You Just Can't Believe in That God Anymore

When we begin our faith with a fear of God, this fear has a way of generalizing into all areas of our existence and even becomes the lens through which we interpret our life's events and assign them meaning. We try to walk carefully inside boundaries not because it's what's best for us, or best for our relationship with God, but because we're afraid of what God will do to us if we stray outside the lines. Try as we might, we all seem to be pretty good at failure, so when hard times come in life, we have a nagging suspicion in the back of our minds that God is somehow punishing us for those times when we just weren't at our personal best. Before we know it, we're trapped in a cycle of fear and misinterpretation that not only pushes us farther away from God, but it sucks the life out of us, leaving us on our spiritual deathbeds.

When I hit my spiritual bottom, I knew I had some decisions to make. Believing in the angry God of my youth didn't work anymore—it was killing the faith inside of me. Yet, I knew I wasn't an atheist or part of any other religion; as my good friend Frank Schaeffer once put it, "I see the creator in Jesus, or I see him nowhere."[2] Thus, both hanging it all up and switching teams were not options for me. If I wanted to be true to myself, and true to what I honestly and sincerely believed, I'd have to relearn how to be Christian, minus the fear-based foundation.

I didn't have all the answers sorted out at that moment; instead, I felt like someone feels on the day he or she decides to finally end a long relationship that isn't working anymore. It was one of those moments where I just threw up my hands and said, "This might be bad timing, I might be totally wrong, and I don't know where I'm going from here, but I'm just done."

The only thing I knew in that moment was that if I believed in God, I believed in a God who was *exactly like Jesus.* When I see Jesus, I see the embodiment of love and compassion; I see a God who loves me, who can empathize with my suffering, and who longs to pull me close, imperfections and all. Jesus is the one who calls me out from the margins and who tells me that despite my flaws and failures, a seat has been saved at his table just for me.

And Jesus is the last person I can imagine setting me on fire for my shortcomings and failures.

I was done with the angry God who hated me and who held hell over my head as if love had a dark side we have to worry about. I was done living in fear, I was done wondering whether I would ever be accepted, and I was done trying to please someone who would have the audacity to burn me alive if I didn't get it right. I was just so effing done.

In my dark moment I knew I had to go one of two ways: die inside, or choose to believe that God is love. One of the best decisions of my life was that I chose love—and love changed everything.

Love Changes Everything

I don't know about you, but in my experience growing up, we would of course affirm what Scripture teaches—that God is love—but there was always a need to qualify the statement. It was never enough to say, "Yes, God is love" and then put a period at the end of the sentence; instead, there always seemed to be a need to add a *but* to the end.

"Yes, God is love, but . . ."

And we certainly had a million buts.

But he's also angry, but he's wrathful, but he's vengeful . . .

Allowing God to be love plus nothing was never enough—it always had to be *love plus something.* And that "something" was usually really, really horrible—it was never love plus mercy but was always love plus wrath, love plus anger, love plus something that *didn't feel loving at all.* Instead of love, and simply love, being our starting point with God—and thus being the foundation upon which the rest of our faith is built—we started building from the idea that love has a secret dark side to it.

In real life, of course, we would never radically redefine love to include so many dark aspects. We would recognize that saying "I love you, but I will take my wrath out on you" would be taking love and adding something to it that does not exist within love. In all honesty, we would likely recognize that our inability to love without all of these other add-ons was actually a result of our sinful nature—our temporary earthly status that makes us almost incapable of loving perfectly without the pale looking glass of sin distorting the pure and unadulterated version of love.

During my time of rethinking God, I began to wonder: What would happen if we stopped adding these dark elements to love, as if love needed to be qualified? What if we recognized that qualifying love with other characteristics, especially negative ones, is simply a reflection of our own inability to express love perfectly? What if we simply believed that God is love, and that this, and this alone, is the *only* possible way to understand or describe God's essence?

I like how Peter Kreeft puts it:

> Love is God's essence. Nowhere else does Scripture express God's essence this way. Scripture says God is just and merciful, but it does not say that God is justice itself or mercy itself. It does say that God is love. . . . Love is God's very essence. Everything else is a manifestation of this essence to us.[3]

Thus, the only possible answer to the question "What is the one word that perfectly describes God?" is *love*.

Pause with me for a moment to think back on the most loving,

healthy relationship you've ever had. Maybe that relationship
was with a grandparent, a parent, a friend, a lover, or a spouse.
What if God's love is like an extreme version of the most loving
relationship you ever had? What if God's love is actually a *perfected
version of the love you received from the one person in your life who
loved you best?*

Call me a heretic (you'll have to get in line behind the Calvinists
if you want to do that, by the way), but I think God actually
is that person, and I think that affirmation is an invitation to
rethink everything we've ever believed about God, believed about
ourselves, and believed about our purpose in life.

Maybe it's time we repent of our fear of God.

I admit, the word "repent" brings up some not-so-feel-good,
fear-based connotations from my upbringing. That was the word
used during all those campfire services where I either asked Jesus
into my heart or "rededicated my life to the Lord." However, the
word "repent" is quite fitting for those of us who find ourselves
trapped in a loveless relationship with God because fear has
stunted the endeavor.

In biblical Greek the word "repent" comes from a military term
similar to the command "about face." During my years in the
military, I knew this term well. When standing in formation and
hearing the preparatory command, "about," and the command
of execution, "face," the entire formation would turn around in
unison. This image of turning around is one that many hellfire
preachers have used when preaching about repentance—except, I
think they were missing an essential element. In those sermons,
repentance is all about "turning away" from sin, and certainly
repentance would include an element of that. However, the deeper
flavor of this word is less about turning *away* from something and
more about turning *toward* something.

So here's my question: As much as the word "repent" makes many of us recoil, what if it is enjoining us to turn *away* from our fear of God and to turn *toward* the love of God?

What if we simply confess that God is love, and then put a period at the end of the sentence? God is love. Period.

Over the years I've watched many people around me fall in love, and thankfully I've had that experience myself. If you've ever fallen in love, you'll understand what I'm about to say: the mutual giving and receiving of love in harmony changes everything about life. Falling in love makes you feel like you've spent your whole life seeing in black and white, but then one day you woke up and saw the brilliance of color. Love makes you realize the dullness of your previous existence and makes you feel alive in places where you didn't even realize you were dead. It jolts you and awakens something inside of you that had been dormant but now blossoms to the point where everything about life seems completely different and full of hope. Love becomes a mirror that invites you to view yourself in a new way—not through the lens of your perceived flaws or imperfections, but through the lens of how love sees you. Love energizes and motivates, giving you a new vision of your future—one that is full of dreams you didn't dare to dream before love awoke a newness of life within you.

Love changes everything and invites you to see yourself, your life, and your purpose in new and beautiful ways.

Repenting of our fears and returning home to the love of God is just like these fleeting, earthly moments where love changed everything. Adding a period to the sentence "God is love" has the power to awaken, inspire, and bring hope—like no other punctuation mark ever could.

Love can, and does, change everything—especially when we affirm that God is love, period, and resist the desire to say anything more.

Starting Over . . . Unafraid

Love always awakens us to a more beautiful reality that we were unable to completely see or grasp before. We know this when it comes to human or romantic relationships, but we often miss this reality when it comes to the realization that God is love. For me, once I decided to believe that God is love—and nothing other than love—I began to see myself, the Bible, the narrative of Scripture, and everything around me in completely new and different ways. I realized that once we embrace being unafraid and apply that reality to God, nothing can remain the same—every single aspect of faith, and life, changes.

I wrestled for some time with what my spiritual path forward would be (I'm one of those internal processors who's always thinking and mulling over possibilities), and it wasn't until Christmas Eve 2015 that everything began to click in place for me. No time of year holds a closer spot in my heart than Christmas. Regardless of the many places where I've been in my spiritual journey, the one thing that has never changed or wavered has been my fascination with the man we call Jesus. Each year at Christmastime, amid the holiday activities, lights, and snow-laden mountains where I live in Maine, I often find myself sitting quietly by my woodstove in the darkness of night and reflecting upon that moment when God finally and personally entered the human story.

At our home we have a tradition: on Christmas Eve I gather the kids around and read the Christmas story from the Gospel of Luke. One year I was cognizant of the many people who were alone over the holidays, so I decided to do a live broadcast over Facebook Mentions of my time reading with my daughter Johanna and my niece, Imani. It was a time of laughter and giggles, and it was extra special to share what was often a private and intimate family moment with so many folks across the Internet. During the broadcast I read the Christmas story with the girls, as I always do. But that year, something hit me differently—and I later found myself sitting by my woodstove in the darkness of Christmas Eve, learning to see everything differently.

When we invite ourselves into the pages of Scripture, we bring with us our questions and tensions, and I am convinced that one of the things that makes Scripture inspired is the way God shows up on those pages to meet us right where we are in that moment. And that year? Well, that moment was no different—the spirit of God was on the pages and met me in the midst of my wrestling. As I sat in the dark, I pondered the reality that when God entered the human story—when he took on flesh and became one of us—the first thing the angel proclaimed to humanity was "Be unafraid!"—as God had arrived to bring great joy to all people.

That is quite different from the ways we're introduced to God, no? I don't think I've ever heard an evangelist begin their message with, "Be unafraid!"

This realization—that Jesus's arrival was proclaimed with the command to "be unafraid"—invited me to ask a new question: If an angel from heaven introduced Jesus with the words "be unafraid," why do some preachers now introduce God with words that are exactly the opposite?

The angel, and the heavenly host that joined that angel, didn't spout a message about God's wrath toward humanity, about his anger with wayward shepherds, or about how he was going to smite those who failed to show hospitality toward the parents of this new baby. Instead, the angel said that the shepherds should be unafraid because God had come to bring great joy to humanity.

There is no reason to fear this God, the angels of heaven remind us.

As I sat beside the crackle of my Christmas Eve fire, it finally sank deep in my spirit that if the story of God began with the command to be unafraid, I should probably just accept and embrace that command.

It also struck me that a beautiful message—truly good news— has been perverted and distorted within much of Americanized Christianity. One simply cannot look at the message of the Franklin Grahams or Ray Comforts of the world and conclude that it's the same message preached by the angels that first Christmas evening.

To paraphrase Samuel L. Jackson in the movie *Pulp Fiction*, it ain't the same ballpark, it ain't the same league, it ain't even the same sport.

When God stepped off his rightful throne and became flesh, the angels didn't announce the coming of a king beset on destroying us.

The angels didn't turn to us and scold us like children, warning that we're "in big trouble now that Dad is here."

The angels didn't announce the arrival of a warrior God who had come to slay his enemies.

Instead, the angels announced the birth of a baby—the Lamb of God, who would take away the sins of the world.

And printed atop the birth announcement of our King were the words "Be unafraid!"

Perhaps this is why so many people are burned out and walking away from Americanized Christianity. Cheap knockoffs never last as long as brand-name products. Sure, you can make something that looks similar and even print the original logo on it, but counterfeits have a way of falling apart after a while.

I think that's what's happening within American Christianity. We've been living a counterfeit version of the real deal for too long, and now the stiches are starting to pop out at the seams. People pick it up and look it over, but then they set it back down, as it daily becomes more obvious that it's just a cheap version of something that was intended to be much better.

The earliest Christians became known as people of "good news," and I often wonder whether they'd recognize many modern American Christians as belonging to the same religion as the one they founded. What began as a message of "good tidings of great joy that will be for *all* people" has somehow become convoluted, distorted, and reduced to a message that's good news for a handful of people, but really bad, absolutely horrible news for the vast majority of us.

A gospel that's good news for a *few* isn't the gospel preached by the angels who announced the arrival of the Promised One. The angels proclaimed that his arrival was good news for *all people.*

Wouldn't it be amazing if Christians today were known as people who always bring good news with them wherever they go?

Might it be that the world is so tired of fear-based doom and gloom associated with the divine that an introduction to God that began with "Be unafraid!" would be like healing balm on an old wound?

I believe Jesus came to start a movement of love that would spread to all the corners of the world and seep deep into every culture it encountered—a movement he simply referred to as "the kingdom." I believe this love is a transforming love, one that purifies and beautifies everything it touches. I believe this transforming love is at the very heart of who God is—because I think Jesus is God made flesh, and that Jesus is the one who walks up to us and begins loving us back to life when we feel dead inside.

And thus, I believe it is part of the core DNA of Christians in all times and places to carry this movement forward—inch by inch, mile by mile, country by country—until love turns the world on its head and transforms the globe into an otherworldly kingdom that is far more glorious and beautiful than anything we could have imagined.

Christians throughout history have faced barriers to carrying this movement forward, and those barriers seem to differ by culture and by generation. For those of us in this present generation, however, one of the primary barriers we must face is ridding the world of fear-based religion in order to introduce everyone to the love-based message of Jesus.

Because it's a beautiful message, and it's one that transforms and changes and stands the test of time.

In order to hear it, all of us in the world must know that God is not distant or angry with us. We must know that God is not a fuming ancient god who needs his fill of blood to contain his wrath. We must know that God is not a volcano god who needs a virgin tossed in from time to time to keep him from blowing his top. We must hear the reality that God is nothing like an ISIS terrorist who sets his enemies ablaze.

No, God is none of these things. God is love.

All of us in the world must come to know the one whom the angels proclaimed. We must know the only one who perfectly reveals to us what God is like and who insisted his arrival be announced with the same words we must learn to speak with great conviction: "Be unafraid!"

Once we do that, I am convinced we'll tip that first domino and find that we begin to see everything—*everything*—differently.

3.

WHEN THE WORD OF GOD ISN'T WHAT YOU THOUGHT IT WAS

Letting go of my fear of God was the natural starting point for me to move toward a healthy faith. Letting go of my ISIS-like god in exchange for a God who must be at *least* half as nice as my next-door neighbor was critical. (My neighbor isn't overly friendly, but I can't imagine he'd ever set me on fire.) However, I quickly realized that exchanging fear for love invited me to begin rethinking everything, and there was no more obvious next step than rethinking the way I (and we) have historically approached the Bible. In fact, when we begin rebuilding a Christian faith that is predicated on love and being unafraid, rethinking our view and approach to Scripture is one of those things that we can't ignore— because it won't let us. When reading Scripture through a lens that says God is love, and nothing else, issues come up—even when we'd rather pretend they aren't there.

For me, revisiting Scripture was critically important. I knew that one of the nonnegotiables in rebuilding my faith was that it had to take the Bible very seriously,[1] but my faith also had to be one that interpreted the Bible through a Jesus lens of *love* instead of *fear*. This love and reverence for the Christian Scriptures is something that goes deep into my childhood, and it isn't something I am willing to let go of.

Bible Champion of the World

Let me tell you something you probably don't know about me: when I was a kid, I was the Bible Champion of the World.

Well, at least I was in my own mind.

I grew up in a small town and quiet farming community in Maine. My grandfather moved there after the end of the Second World War and nicknamed our property "Dunlookin Farm" because, as the story goes, when he first saw the property and the 1852 barn, he realized he was "dunlookin" for a place to settle and build a life—so, he settled and built a life. The hunger for small-town farming life must be hereditary, because my father continued the family trade and to this day still milks his herd of organic Holsteins and Jerseys twice daily.

Our town didn't have much; when I say "small town," I really mean *small town*. We didn't have a traffic light, a grocery store, or even a gas station—those were all things you had to go "into town" to see (and by "into town," we meant the next town over). And entertainment? Other than when the cows got out (those stories could fill their own book), the only entertainment we had was entertainment we *made*. What we did have, however, was a small community church called the East Wilton Union Church—and at least for my family, that church was the center of small-town living.

The quiet church, with faded white paint and stained-glass

windows that weren't too Catholic-y (we didn't think Catholics were real Christians, and I assume whoever built the building didn't want anyone getting confused), was situated right off of the main street that went through town. Back then, we were old school. We didn't have fog machines, a worship band (though we did have "special music," when people sang along with a cassette tape), or many of the other things one might find in a church these days; but we were in church Sunday mornings, Sunday evenings, and we even had prayer meetings on Wednesday nights (surely I'm not the only one who grew up going to Wednesday-night prayer meetings). And in the summer? Well, you guessed it—in the summer we had us some mighty fine Vacation Bible School.

One summer a couple of missionaries came to town and offered to conduct VBS for the church that year. They were two young guys who rode everywhere on bikes and wore navy-blue slacks (did I just say "slacks"?), white button-down shirts, and navy-blue ties. Seriously, they wore this same outfit every day. In retrospect, they sure did look like a couple of Mormons, so I'm surprised the church agreed to let them host summer programming. Yet, host they did—and instead of VBS, they called it the Neighborhood Bible Time. I don't remember a single lesson they taught that summer, but I do remember it was epic on two counts: pies to the face, and all of those ribbons.

On the first day of VBS—sorry, I mean Neighborhood Bible Time—the leaders announced an "incentive program" of sorts. The first appealed to everyone, but the second appealed especially to me. The first incentive was golden: on the final day of the program everyone who had perfect attendance would get to smash a pie in the face of one of the leaders—and, get this: *the only rule was that the pie had to be made out of food.* Now, I have been a Creative Rule Navigator since my earliest days, so when they said "food," I immediately realized that word was open to a world of nuance and interpretation.

I knew that perfect attendance on my end was a done deal—there was no way I was passing up that kind of opportunity. From that point on, I attended Neighborhood Bible Time each day in the afternoons, but I spent my mornings scouring the farm for any rotten vegetables I could find. I searched the basement, dug up stuff from the garden, and even went through the trash a few times—I was a ten-year-old boy on a mission. By the end of the week I had a "pie" that consisted of rotten eggs and a whole bunch of stuff that normally would have been tossed into the pasture to rot or be eaten by the cows. In fact, I didn't even know what some of the stuff was—I just knew it was gross, but it technically could be classified as "food." Thus, I was well within the rules.

On the last day when I saw that other kids had brought chocolate cream, lemon meringue, and totally normal, nongross pies, I was so proud of my creativity that I could hardly contain my excitement. And, let me tell you: when the leaders told us we couldn't throw the pies, for safety reasons, but instead had to walk up and slowly rub the pies in their faces, I felt the Holy Spirit quietly confirm in my heart that this was the best idea I had ever had.

But rotten pies aside, that wasn't the incentive I was the most excited about.

Along with announcing the pie-to-the-face incentive, the same guys who rode their ten-speeds (remember those?—before mountain bikes) in those navy slacks also showed us a box full of ribbons of every color you could imagine—red, blue, green—and each one even had that fancy gold lettering on it. However, these were no ordinary ribbons. No secret-recipe pie in a baking contest could win you one; nor could you earn one from winning a race. These ribbons were different.

These were ribbons you could only win for memorizing Bible verses.

As soon as I laid my eyes on them, I knew those ribbons were going to be mine. Just as I knew that my perfect attendance and the rotten pie was a done deal, I knew in the recesses of my soul that those ribbons would be on my chest by week's end—because *memorizing the Bible was my bag,* as they say. I had never won a ribbon for anything in my life—I was small and slow without many talents, but if it could be said that I did have a talent, *memorizing Bible verses was it.*

My friends had their own gifts and talents—Albert could make fart sounds with his armpit, and John could throw a ball higher in the air than any of the other kids—but *I was the King of Bible Memorization.* In fact, I was the kid who could make a room groan when someone shouted out "Sword drill!" because if my quick fingers didn't get me to the right Bible verse first, I could often shout it out from memory (which eventually was declared as being unfair to others).

This was my thing, and *these ribbons were my moment.*

I knew it.

I showed up with the verse of the day memorized every time—I knew those suckers cold. I quickly got bored with the daily ribbons to be won, so I started asking about other ribbons that weren't being advertised, such as the really, really big one you could get for memorizing the Ten Commandments or for memorizing all the books of the Bible in the correct order.

And so I memorized those suckers cold, too.

Most of the other kids couldn't have cared less about those ribbons, but for some reason, they mattered to me. I made sure I memorized every possible verse, and by the end of the week I had been awarded nearly all the ribbons. I was so proud that I pinned them all to my chest with safety pins and paraded around the church lawn in a post–Neighborhood Bible Time victory lap. I imagine I must have looked like a three-foot-high field general of some sort—one with his chest weighed down with medals given for battles won.

What can I say? Memorizing the Bible was my thing, and to me, I was the Bible Champion of the World.

Getting the Blankets Pulled Off

Since the days of my youth, I have always loved the Bible—in fact, I grew up to become a preacher and teacher of the Bible, even going so far as graduating seminary *three times* and ultimately becoming a doctor of Jesus-y and Bible-type stuff. The youthful love and excitement I had for it—and all the stuff inside it—never quite left me.

Someone once asked the twentieth-century British evangelist Rodney Smith why he spent so much of his life traveling and preaching (some estimate he crossed the Atlantic about forty-five times to preach in the United States). After thinking about it, Smith simply replied, "Because I've never lost the wonder of it all." The way Smith felt about traveling and preaching is how I feel about the Bible: there's an aspect of awe and wonder about it that keeps drawing me back.

Although I am no longer the boy parading around the church lawn with a chest full of Scripture-memorization ribbons, that boy still exists somewhere inside me—and he's never quite lost the wonder of it all.

At least, not *totally*.

As with all relationships, my relationship with the Bible has grown and changed, faced ups and downs, matured through hardship, and had moments of both excitement and tremendous disappointment. Like a spouse who looks at his or her partner after thirty years of marriage and thinks, *This isn't the same person I married—and I think I'm actually okay with that,*" I still love the Bible—but I love it differently from how I once loved it.

Many marriages fall on challenging times when one partner starts to *really* get to know the other and rediscovers flaws that were once so easily dismissed or overlooked while dating (we have a tremendous ability to do that, don't we?). In the same way, somewhere between learning to understand Greek and raising children, my relationship with the Bible faced similar moments when I noticed something that needed to be dealt with, but like a love-stricken suitor, I chose the path of looking the other way.

Now, here's an important truth: how we face conflict and tension in life's critical moments can alter the entire trajectory of our lives. Whether it is our relationship with our spouse, our relationships with our children, or even our relationship with God, the decisions we make in these tense moments become some of the most important decisions we'll ever make.

What is also true is that many of us have an unhealthy tendency to pretend these moments are not staring us in the face. Like children who pull the blankets over their heads to hide and ignore what's on the other side of those blankets, we somehow persuade ourselves that ignoring the tension and conflict will make it all go away. Unfortunately, it doesn't. I've honestly never seen total conflict avoidance produce anything good—certainly not in my own life.

Life underneath the blankets may be comfortable and give us the illusion that our world is intact, but the longer we ignore what is happening on the other side of this false world, the more tension and discontent amass under the surfaces of our lives. This avoidance technique (one I have mastered in life, trust me on that) only helps us avoid for so long, as a moment comes in these relationships (even in relationship with ourselves) where the blankets are unsuspectingly pulled off our heads. When that moment comes, we're forced to finally face the things we hadn't been ready to see—or things we weren't comfortable admitting we'd seen.

Life has a way of saying, "Ready or not, here I come!"

When the blankets get pulled off, we're faced with an unexpected explosion of reality that forces us to finally look conflict in the face, and to make a choice about which path we are going to travel in response. The potential options may be plentiful, but once the blankets get pulled off our heads, there's one option that's no longer on the table: *avoidance*.

When it came to the Bible and me, I had spent years soaking up information, but I had also spent too much time putting the blankets over my head and pretending I hadn't seen some things that I'd rather have not seen. The long season of avoidance came to a swift end one night while reading Bible stories with my daughter Johanna. This de-blanketing moment, when I finally realized that avoidance was no longer an option, came when she asked me a simple question after reading about the war conquests in the Old Testament: "Daddy, why did God tell them to kill all their enemies' babies and even their pets?"

Yikes! When I was still the King of Bible Memorization, these stories hadn't been a problem for me. The image of God as a brutal warrior who commanded his people to have no mercy on their enemies—slaughtering men, women, babies, and *even puppies*—seemed like a powerful and awesome God (looking back, I have no idea how I arrived at that conclusion). But here was the problem for my daughter Johanna: ever since she jumped into my arms in Chincha, Peru, and called me "Daddy" for the first time (back then she actually called me "Papi"), I had been teaching her that God is the most loving being her mind could ever imagine—and she believed me. But now she was being introduced to God the Puppy Slayer, and that version of God simply didn't jibe with her spirit—because she already knew what God was like: he was just like Jesus.

As I pondered her question, I realized that she and I were facing the same dilemma: continue to affirm and believe that God is exactly like Jesus, or engage in the false religion of Biblicism that forces us to affirm that every conflicting description of God in the Bible is somehow as equally accurate a revelation of God as is the revelation of God in the person of Jesus.

I knew the blankets had been pulled off my head and that there was no going back to the cozy, false world I had created where everything in the Bible made perfect sense. It was one thing to ignore my own questions about the Bible, but as a father I knew that ignoring this question from my daughter could plant countless seeds of doubt in her surrounding God's character and nature—doubts that could have given birth to a lot of fear. I could remain neutral no longer; I had to choose between love and fear. So, I answered her: "God didn't tell them to kill all the babies and even their pets. They just *thought* God said that, because they hadn't met Jesus yet."

As I tucked her in that evening, I became keenly aware that there were some things about the Bible that I no longer believed—at least, I no longer believed we were supposed to interpret or understand them the way we have often been taught. I knew I had to take my new mission to be unafraid beyond just God. I needed to face these things that I no longer believed about

the Bible so that I could move forward in discovering what I
actually *did* believe.

Trinity No More: The False Religion of Biblicism

Those of us who find ourselves curled up with blankets over our
heads when it comes to the Bible most likely ended up in that
position because we fell prey to a dangerous and toxic religion
called "Biblicism." In fact, Biblicism is more than just a false
religion; Biblicism is by nature anti-Christ because it so often
stands opposed to the ways of Jesus.

The historic, orthodox Christian religion is Trinitarian in
nature, holding that God exists through three persons: God
the Father, God the Son, and God the Holy Spirit. The heresy of
Biblicism, however, promulgates the functional belief in a *four-
person* Godhead rather than belief in the Trinity. Sure, Biblicism
promotes belief in God the Father, God the Son, and God the Holy
Spirit—but it includes a dangerous *fourth* person: God the Holy
Scriptures.

The religion of Biblicism is founded upon the idea that
Christians are people who follow the Bible, because in Biblicism,
the Bible itself becomes God. In fact, Biblicism even has its own
clearly defined brand and often uses code words like "biblical
worldview" or just plain "biblical" to distinguish itself from other
types of belief systems or even from other Christians (and now
we're starting to get at why Ken Ham blocked me on Facebook).
For Biblicists, the entire Bible is the inerrant Word of God and
the foundation and final authority for all matters in life. As the
former King of Bible Memorization and Sword Drill Champion
of El Mundo, I admit that this sounds good and beautiful on the

surface—until the blankets get pulled off and we realize that *a religion based on following the Bible can mean almost anything we want it to mean.* All we have to do is consider the reality that religion rooted in "following the Bible" has led to the establishment of more than forty thousand versions of the Christian religion around the world. I mean, if following the Bible—what Biblicists claim is God's inerrant word—is as straightforward as it sounds, wouldn't that lead to *one* religion instead of forty thousand?

At the heart of why Biblicism is so dangerous is its malleable nature: it can be bent and shaped into almost any form. I believe this is because the Bible typically used in the religion of Biblicism is composed of sixty-six books that were written by various authors from different times and places. In it we find writings that come from vastly different contexts, different languages, different literary genres. Essentially, the Bible is less of a book and more of a library of writings containing as much diversity as one can imagine. This diversity is beautiful and can have a life-giving function, but it's dangerous when the diversity is approached through a lens of Biblicism that sees every story told, every word written, as the inerrant Word of God. One would think that viewing every word of Scripture as a clear and perfect word from God would make things simpler, but it actually achieves the opposite: it unnecessarily forces people to pick and choose among the tensions and conflicts found in the Bible.

In Biblicism, developing a "biblical" worldview is almost like a "choose your own adventure" book. If you don't like a lesson derived from one part of the Bible, you can usually find something from a different part to justify a dissenting view. Since Biblicism claims that the whole Bible, every word, is the inerrant Word of God, when tension or apparent disagreement is seen in Scripture, there is *no mechanism to break the tie* or resolve the conflict.

How do you break a tie or resolve tension when neither side has authority over the other? This is precisely why we have so many different versions of the Christian religion in disagreement with one another, with each one claiming that the authority of the Bible is on *their* side: we read the Bible as if every voice in it has equal authority and then walk away with mixed messages that we're told are supposed to mesh in harmony with one another—but they don't. So, we put the blankets over our heads and try to be good Christians who don't ask hard questions—because who are we to question God's perfect word?

Biblicism always results in division and frustration because it lacks direction and has no way to resolve inner conflict. Let's think of it this way: Imagine playing a game where everyone has different goals, each player (and team) emphasizes different rules, and there are no referees to settle disputes. Such a game would quickly dissolve into chaos—which is exactly what happens within Biblicism. Except in the latter, it's not simply chaos—instead it's a long history of killing one another over our disagreements about the Bible. Although these days it's illegal to literally burn people at the stake (perhaps the only reason why you don't see this happening in the United States), we have plenty of modern ways to figuratively burn people at the stake when they disagree with our take on the Bible—and these modern ways of burning can hurt just as much as the old way of dealing with heretics.

If the fruits of Biblicism are division and frustration, the end result is a total state of physical and spiritual exhaustion. While I have always been fascinated with the Bible, living out the religion of Biblicism nearly wrecked my faith, because the nature of Biblicism requires you to run in circles until you eventually collapse. Every time you think you've found an answer, another Biblicist seems to be telling you, "Yes, but you have to take into account the *whole* Word of God, so you're wrong." Eventually you slump back into your bed, pull the blankets over your head, and ask yourself, "If this is all God's Word, shouldn't it be a little less confusing?"

I am convinced that the heresy of Biblicism is simply a case of misidentification—but one that leads to the destructive idolatry of the Trinity + 1. This idolatry stems from the mistake we have made: calling a collection of writings the "Word of God" and completely missing the reality that *Jesus alone is the Word of God*.

The Word of God isn't a book—it's a person.

In the opening verse of John's Gospel he tells us, "In the beginning was the Word, and the Word was with God and the Word was God." John then tells us that everything in existence was created *by the Word* and that eventually the Word *became a human being* and walked among us. If the collection of writings we call the Bible is the Word of God, based upon the opening of John we'd also have to say that the Bible has always existed, the Bible created everything in the cosmos, the Bible became flesh and walked among us, and the Bible itself *is God*. I'm sorry, but that just *breeeeeeeds* fear-based religion. When we place the Bible on equal footing with God, we become paralyzed by how to deal with it—because any criticism of the Bible becomes criticism of God himself.

The cure for the religion of Biblicism is the realization that *Jesus* is the inerrant Word of God, and the Bible is just a collection of inspired and useful writings that *introduce us to him*. To miss this is to miss the entire point: the Bible is not a flat book, and it is not a path without a destination; the Bible is a book that leads somewhere, it's a book that has a purpose and a point—and *that point has always been introducing us to Jesus*. Trading the main thing for that which points to the thing is a tragic mistake that leads us to a totally different religion from the religion of Jesus.

Let me be clear: whenever we find tension between something Jesus taught and something taught elsewhere in the Bible, the tiebreaker always goes to Jesus. *Always.*

Rethinking Old Descriptions

In the spring of 2011 I found myself in a Peruvian orphanage. Although I had taken plenty of mission trips during my youth that included visits to orphanages, this one was different: this was the day that I was to become a dad. The orphanage was situated on the outskirts of town at the end of a long dirt road that had gullies on both sides. These gullies were filled with smoldering and burning trash, giving the area a unique stench that followed us all the way to the main building. When we pulled up to the building, we easily could have mistaken it for a prison because it had high cement walls and even a guard tower hovering over it. My senses were in overload at those moments, but I could think of only one thing: I just wanted to see my girls. As the big steel doors to the compound opened, I finally saw them—standing at a distance, waving to us through the bars of what can only be described as a cell door. With shouts of "¡Estamos aquí!" the day quickly became a beautiful blur of tears and laughter . . . and life hasn't been the same since.

That day was the first time I met my daughters face-to-face, but it was not the first day that I had any knowledge of what they were like. Long before we set foot in Peru, my wife and I had gone through a long and expensive journey to complete the adoption. As part of that process, we had received files on our daughters that contained information—school records, medical records, and other useful reports—that the adoption agency thought we needed to know. Since we had not yet met our daughters in person, these reports of others' observations and interpretations of our daughters' personalities and needs were the only things we had to go on. For a time, we made decisions based on what other people had observed of our children, but we quickly realized that once you get to know someone, *you have to reinterpret all the things that were said about that person in the past.*

After some time getting to know our daughters, we recognized that at times the old documents did a good job of describing who they were, but at other times, the descriptions and interpretations conflict with our personal experiences of our daughters. For example, when we received the school records for one of them, we saw written across the top a horrid label that simply read "Non-learner." We had no idea what this could mean but soon realized she had some barriers that were preventing her from accessing all the facets of school. After she was properly examined and evaluated, however, we discovered the deeper truth: she had a complex form of dyslexia. Once the proper supports were put in place, it quickly became clear that she wasn't a "non-learner" at all—she simply learned things differently from other kids. Through this, and other similar experiences, my wife and I realized that the more we got to know our children in person, the more we had to reevaluate and reinterpret the observations others had made of them in the past. The information in the old documents wasn't always wrong or misleading, but it didn't always match the way we experienced our daughters day-to-day, either. These old documents were useful, but they provided *limited* observations at best and at times proved to be unintentionally misleading in describing who I now know my children to be.

Their mom and I still hold onto these old documents and find them to have value, but they are no substitute for our children in the flesh. Sometimes we refer back to them to see whether we might learn something from them when comparing them to our own observations of our kids. At other times, we reinterpret the information contained in them in light of what we now know to be true from our personal interactions with our children. But here's what we don't do: *we don't allow the old records to define who our children are.* They are who they are in the flesh—that is what is *ultimately true of them.* Everything else? Well, everything else needs to be revaluated and reinterpreted in relation to the ultimate truth and the ultimate reality revealed in their actual personhood. Attempted descriptions of people must never be confused or allowed to trump the people themselves.

Just as with my daughters, what Jesus taught versus what is taught elsewhere in Scripture, and portraits of God from some portions of the Old Testament versus the image of God in Jesus, are not a case of equals. Jesus is the Word of God, the wisdom of God, and the exact representation of God's essence. Thus, Jesus reigns supreme over everything—including the Bible itself. And since Jesus models perfect love, the very essence of what God is like, I knew that life beyond a fear-based faith had to be built not just upon love, but upon the teachings of the one who loves perfectly.

The Bible Isn't a Swiss Army Knife

Having the blankets pulled off our heads can be a traumatic moment in our faith journey. For some of us, this might end the journey entirely, as we come to realize that the Bible might not work exactly as we were taught it works. This certainly presents a compelling temptation to walk away, something I'm grateful I didn't do. New Testament scholar Pete Enns refers to this as the Bible "not behaving the way we want it to behave,"[2] but I think for me it is less about wanting the Bible to behave in a certain way and more about a realization that it doesn't work the way I was taught it works.

After years as a preacher and Bible teacher, I found the process of interpreting the Bible from the perspective of every description of God being equally true and accurate to be exhausting. The Bible simply didn't harmonize in the way I was taught it harmonized, and trying to make it do so was a daunting task. I was burned out. I was so burned out that I fell into the trap that President Barack Obama's spiritual adviser, Joshua DuBois, warns about— the trap of becoming a "professional Christian." I continued to engage the Bible every day because it was my job, *not* because I was experiencing life, growth, or transformation because of it. I eventually reached the point where I found myself dreading any engagement with the Bible, because I had long since realized that the Bible doesn't do what I had been taught it does and I was no longer able to see the Bible the way I saw it back when I was the Bible Champion of the World. I had yet to find an alternative way of working with the Bible that satisfied *both* my heart and my conscience. But I did know this: I no longer believed that the Bible was some perfect love letter from God where every word was on an equal footing, as if God had written it himself in one sitting— because I had spent a lifetime trying to use it that way, and it had never worked.

But then I wondered: Maybe I was simply using the Bible in the wrong way?

I don't have a lot of memories of my grandfather because I was just nine years old when he died, but I'm thankful that I do have some. A descendant of Danish immigrants (our family name is Hedegard), he spent thirty years in the military before retiring and starting an upholstery business in his basement. Instead of being a spacious workspace, the basement was cluttered with old chairs, fabric, tacks of every design imaginable, and a myriad of tools. Oh, I loved screwing around with his tools.

I didn't turn out to be a carpenter like my grandfather, and I'm not all that handy (if they don't find you handy, make sure they find you handsome—so at least I scored there), but from watching him work, I learned that tools have a pretty specific function. For example, a hammer might be great for pounding nails, but it's not so great for sawing wood or turning screws. But in the case of the Swiss Army knife, it can be *whatever you want it to be.*

The religion of Biblicism is rooted in the idea that the Bible is a Swiss Army knife, where all pieces are equal and yet existing for a thousand different uses. This, of course, gets us into all sorts of trouble (like more than forty thousand versions of trouble) because this isn't how the Bible works. The Bible isn't a book that reveals the answers to all of life's deepest and most pressing questions. It's not a book that gives us clear-cut guidance on what to do in each and every life circumstance. It's not an owner's manual that tells us everything we need to know about life. We can try to use it this way, but we will have as much luck as we would have trying to use a hammer to saw a piece of timber in a straight line. It's just not what it was designed to do.

Whether we like it or not, the Bible isn't an all-purpose tool with a thousand functions; the Bible is a collection of divinely inspired writings with *one, single purpose:* to introduce us to Jesus Christ, the Word of God. And, once we meet him, the goal is to *learn to become like him.* That's what the Bible does. Thinking it does anything else is like trying to use a hammer to saw a piece of timber.

The problems we run into with the Bible are often resolved once we embrace viewing it as a tool with a very *specific function*. If the entire point of the Bible is to introduce readers to Jesus, and if the entire goal of Scripture is to transform readers into being like Jesus, we no longer find ourselves feeling the need to huddle in a bed with blankets over our heads when we find things that clearly don't agree with what we see in Jesus. Instead of the false binary options of running from the Bible or trying to make all the voices in the Bible harmonize like a well-practiced choir, we are faced with the invitation to reinterpret everything in light of Jesus—because that's actually how even Jesus engaged with Scripture. In the story of Jesus walking on the road to Emmaus (Luke 24:13–27), he explains to Cleopas and his companion that all the law and the prophets point to him. Similarly in John 5:39–40 we see Jesus pointing out that while the religious teachers knew Scripture inside and out, they still didn't realize that the entire purpose of Scripture was to reveal himself. So even Jesus saw the Old Testament as needing to be reinterpreted in a new way that had not been done before.

There's a divide between how Jesus engaged with Scripture and how Biblicism engages with it. This isn't new: Biblicism is similar to the religion of the Pharisees during the time of Jesus, because the Pharisees were book-centered, not Jesus-centered. There are multiple times in the ministry of Jesus when we see him inviting his listeners to consider a deeper truth: it is possible to be so biblically oriented that we don't recognize God, even when he is walking right beside us. Jesus tries to clue them in to what they were missing, pointing out that although they knew the Bible inside and out, they were missing the reality that the entire purpose of the Hebrew Scriptures is to introduce people to Jesus and to extend the invitation to be like him. But even when Jesus practically drew them a freaking picture, they were still unable to pick up what he was laying down.

These were people who literally walked with God.

They knew what Jesus looked like, what his voice sounded like, and even his tiniest facial expressions. Yet, God made flesh was so different from what they expected, and so different from the warrior portraits of God they knew from the Hebrew Scriptures, that they *didn't recognize they were talking to the ultimate revelation of God.* They had been following the book instead of following the person—and the book and the person don't always mirror one another. Every time I read of this encounter in the New Testament, I am reminded that *it is entirely possible to be so busy trying to follow the Bible that a person never actually ends up following Jesus.*

Let that sink in for a moment: the only time in human history when God walked in the flesh and revealed himself to humanity, the people who knew Scripture backward and forward—like Biblicists today—still couldn't recognize God even when he walked with them and talked to them.

In fact, *the Biblicists of the time—the Pharisees—were the ones who repeatedly wanted him dead.*

You see, Jesus doesn't call us to a life of becoming progressively more and more like the Bible. Jesus calls us to a life of becoming more and more like *him.* The Bible is simply the vehicle to make the introduction.

The goal has never been for us to live biblically. The goal has always been for us to live like Christ—and there is a massive difference between these two options.

For those who grow up in this false religion, that's an easy reality to miss. It happened back then, and it's still happening today—because when we treat the Bible like a Swiss Army knife, it becomes *the thing itself* instead of *that which points us to the thing*.

Why Biblicism Is the Most Popular Christian-ish Religion in America

If Biblicism is holding us back from truly knowing God, then why do we still use this approach to religion? We can start to answer this question by looking at the crucifixion. On the day that Jesus was killed, he almost received a last-minute stay of execution. The Roman governor, Pilate, had no desire to have Jesus crucified and even attested that he couldn't find any fault with Jesus. However, the crowd was not pleased when Pilate wavered on their demands that Jesus be put to death, so Pilate tried to find a way out. He ultimately decided to offer the crowd a choice, which stems from a tradition of pardoning a prisoner at Passover. He offered the crowd the choice of Jesus or Barabbas.

The Gospel writers don't seem to question the guilt of Barabbas. In fact, Matthew notes that Barabbas was a notorious criminal— his face and his infamous deeds would have been well-known to the crowd. For Pilate (and Jesus) this choice *should* have been a slam dunk: a man who had done no wrong and was famous for healing the sick, versus a man known for his violent deeds. However, with the angry shouts of the crowd, Pilate realized that this plan had failed and the people had picked Barabbas over Jesus.

Two thousand years ago, the crowd made their decision and shouted, "Give us Barabbas!" And although he goes by different names these days, people are still picking Barabbas over Jesus.

Such is the nature of the religion of Biblicism. But instead of picking something or someone evil over Jesus, Biblicism is far more cunning: it picks this idea of following *the Bible* over following Jesus and thus is able reject him with a deep sense of piety and religious superiority.

People have been running away from Jesus since the beginning. The Gospels tell us that at certain points of his ministry, people found his teachings troubling and that many of his disciples completely abandoned him (John 6:63–66). We see the rich young ruler who *said* he wanted to follow Jesus, but after surveying the cost, he "went away grieving." And of course, we see Jesus in the Garden of Gethsemane being led away in chains as his friends scattered.

Rejecting Jesus and running from him is nothing new—and using Scripture as a getaway car isn't either. But in this case, instead of walking away sad or fleeing the garden, using Scripture to avoid Jesus is a path where one can do the fleeing quite publicly, and while feeling good about it in the process.

This is why the religion of Biblicism has replaced so much of Christianity in the United States today: if you want to run and hide from the ways of Jesus, one of the most self-righteous paths you can take is *to use the Bible to do it.* Those who do this are not Christians—they are Biblicists.

Why would you want to hide from Jesus? Different people have different reasons, but in the American context I think that it has something to do with the fact that Jesus was antiwar, and preached total nonviolence; he radically included people whom the religious elite considered the "worst of sinners"; he was a feminist; he told people to pay their taxes; he was against the death penalty; he warned those who refused to welcome immigrants, feed the hungry, and clothe the naked that they would face eternal judgment; and he taught that it was nearly impossible for rich people to enter his kingdom. So, I'll let you connect the dots on why Americanized Christianity thrives on Biblicism instead of Jesus. Biblicists find that following Jesus is far too costly for them; but unlike those ancient teachers of the law, today's Biblicists do not have the courage to simply walk away and be honest about their rejection of him.

Biblicism leads to its own brand of religion, and it happens innocently enough. When we're taught that the entire Bible is the Word instead of being taught that Jesus alone is the Word and our final authority for living, every word of Scripture *appears* to sit on equal footing with every word from the mouth of Jesus. Every word in the Bible, not just the words with red letters, becomes something Jesus said—the inerrant Word of God. Instead of Jesus being the "exact imprint of God's very being" (Heb 1:3), every attempted portrait of God becomes an exact imprint of God— which is precisely how we end up faced with the conflict between God the Enemy-Lover and God the Puppy Slayer. In Biblicism, every action attributed to God becomes something God *actually did,* and every word on every page is something God *actually said.* This mindset is where Biblicism presents an enticing invitation to run away from Jesus when we find something we don't like or that sounds too costly—and it allows us to actually thump Jesus with the Bible itself.

Thumping Jesus with the Bible, the hallmark identifier of a Biblicist, usually comes in the form of "yeah, buts" much in the same way Biblicists try to qualify "God is love." Not able or willing to simply accept and obey the teachings of Jesus, Biblicists need to qualify Jesus and put him in his place—a classic process of trying to find a loophole in something when we don't have the simple courage to openly admit that we just don't agree with Jesus. Thus, we interpret Jesus with Scripture instead of interpreting Scripture with Jesus, and we express that in the form of these yeah, buts.

For example, Christians will say, "Jesus commanded us to love our enemies and to not repay evil with violence." Biblicists, knowing their Bible well, will respond with a host of yeah, buts:

> Yeah, but Jesus was the same person who commanded Israel in the Old Testament to slaughter their enemies.

> Yeah, but David killed Goliath, and he was the apple of God's eye.

> Yeah, but God himself killed off most of humanity in the flood.

> Yeah, but Jesus is coming back and is going to kill his enemies, so clearly he didn't mean we couldn't kill them ourselves.

Or, without actually backing up their positions, Biblicists will often just look at you indignantly and say, "Yeah, but I believe *all of Scripture*."

We do this with many things Jesus taught, not just the issue of loving our enemies. The better we know our Bible, the easier it is to justify not doing what Jesus did or following what he taught. His commands for practicing mercy, generosity, forgiveness, and self-sacrifice just aren't a good fit for propping up the American dream and the American way of life, so we reject the religion of Jesus in favor of a religion that can be bent and shaped to give the *illusion* that the American way is God's way.

Biblicists will also creatively use Scripture to suit themselves—forcefully applying some texts to everyone else while resisting the same application to their own lives. For example, a Biblicist might say, "You can't be gay and be a Christian." But when I respond with, "Well, Jesus said you couldn't be a Christian if you don't help the poor and welcome immigrants," that same Biblicist will turn around and say, "You teach a works-based salvation, heretic." Instead of being consistent, Biblicists become like the Pharisees of old—people of a circular, convoluted, book-based religion who can look God in the face and *still not recognize him.*

It wasn't until my daughter confronted me with the choice between the loving Jesus and God the Puppy Slayer that I began to fully appreciate how important the ways we interpret the Bible are and how they inform our ideas of God.

I believe that for those of us in a fear-based faith, we have fallen prey to following a book-based religion that has us running in a thousand different directions instead of the one, single direction the Bible is designed to point us: toward Jesus. Jesus himself claimed to be the one true vine from which all life stems, and when we attempt to find life, meaning, or identity from anything else—even the Bible—we find ourselves separated from the only thing that can truly bring life.

Beyond Biblicism: A Better Way Forward

Moving beyond God the Puppy Slayer toward a God who is much more Christlike, while also honoring the inspiration of Scripture, can seem like a daunting task. However, as I began to rework my faith, I discovered that this task is, in fact, entirely possible. Not only is it possible, but reclaiming the love I had for Scripture as a child, with the God I found in Jesus, actually makes everything more beautiful, not less.

When I think back to my days as the King of Bible Memorization, I remember that I often memorized Scripture by individual verses that were either written out on index cards or were part of one of those Bible memorization flash-card sets. This verse-by-verse approach to Scripture worked for me in terms of memorization, but it became a problem once I started to mature my spiritual perspectives. This approach isolates the verses from the grander narrative, which distorts the grander lessons of the Bible.

This is when it's important to remember that the Bible is a series of stories. And stories aren't good stories when everything is clear in the beginning of the narrative; good stories are those where we come to progressively know and understand the characters and plot over the course of the story. Good authors pay attention to character development and narrative arc, which allows readers to slowly peel back the story's layers to fully understand what is happening and who the characters are as complex individuals. The story we see unfold in the Bible is not that different from what we find in a good novel: as the story progresses, we get clearer and clearer glimpses of the true identity of the main character.

So how do we read the Old Testament as part of the larger, Jesus-based narrative? How does this part of the Bible point toward a Christian faith that is rooted in Jesus if he wasn't around yet? To answer this, it's important to remember that Israel's story is a story of being *in the process of getting to know God,* all before Jesus presents himself as the ultimate revelation of God. It is not unlike other relationships where we need time to fully understand and appreciate the true self and identity of the other person in the relationship. The story involves moments when Israel truly sees

God, and moments when they profoundly misunderstand God—both of which are normal parts of any relationship.

For example, Israel had assumed that this Living God was like the other bloodthirsty gods around them and that he needed ritual sacrifice to help keep his anger in check. However, we find in the New Testament book of Hebrews that this system was something God never desired, that it never worked, and that he took no pleasure in it. In this way, we see that not everything in the Old Testament is a perfect representation of who God is or what God desires. It's a story of people who are getting to know God, and that includes glimpses of both his true character and nature as well as what Paul calls "shadows" where God was clearly misunderstood.

Often we are presented with false binary options of either (a) accepting that everything in the Old Testament is inerrant and a perfect representation of God's desires or character, or (b) approaching the Old Testament in a dismissive way (the heresy of Marcionism, which I reject). I believe this is predicated on a faulty doctrine of inerrancy, which gives us these false options. Inerrancy is based upon the claims of 2 Timothy 3:16, which ironically doesn't claim inerrancy at all: what the verse actually says is that all Scripture is inspired and *useful* ("All scripture is inspired by God and is useful for teaching, for reproof, for correction, and for training in righteousness").

There's a big difference between being *inerrant* and being *useful*. The Old Testament narrative can be one that is both inspired and useful without it perfectly revealing the exact representation of what God is like in every portrait a particular author makes. Much like the way I now view the preadoption records of my daughters, we find the old records useful inasmuch as we compare them to fleshly reality. In this way, I find it helpful to ask a new set of questions now when I read the Old Testament:

- How does this passage or story point us toward Jesus, directly or symbolically?

- What did Jesus teach on this issue? Did he affirm this principle, clarify it, or overturn it?

- How is this passage, event, or story useful in illuminating the teachings of Jesus?

- If the people in this story were to meet God in the flesh and have access to the teachings and example of Jesus, how might they handle the situation differently? How might they handle it in the same way?

When we return to viewing the Old Testament not as a perfect representation of God's character but as a story that is *useful* in pointing us to Jesus, a world of options opens up to us in between the false choices that are often presented to us.

- Is it not useful to invite yourself into a beautiful story of two people who are getting to know each other and who are going to do beautiful things together?

- Is not useful to stand from the outside and see where mistakes are made and where misunderstandings happen?

- Is it not useful to see a beautiful story unfolding where all the questions about the true nature and personality of the main character will finally be revealed in a major, climactic revelation of identity?

I find this new way of viewing the Old Testament as something that enhances, not diminishes, my love for it. It is a story of Israel *getting to know God* and one that climaxes in a beautiful moment when God shows up and becomes one of them. Perhaps what I find most exciting about this unfolding story is that when God shows up, he not only clarifies misunderstandings but also gives the people a new example of how they ought to live—one that is very, very different from the old way of living. In fact, God made flesh actually calls adopting this new way of living being "born all over again."

And this is what it means to be born again: to reject book-based religion and to follow Jesus instead.

The heretical religion of American Biblicism, while having the aura of piety and righteousness, rejects the call of Jesus to be born again and to follow in his ways. What American Biblicists have failed to realize is that one can follow Jesus, or one can follow the "whole Bible," but one cannot follow both at the same time. The first, Jesus, is the inerrant Word of God and the wisdom of God, while the second, the Bible, is a collection of inspired writings that reveal to us how this Word became known to us.

Biblicism will likely always be popular in America, as it's a great companion for justifying so much of the "American way of life." There are more than twenty-three thousand verses in the Old Testament, and among them nearly anyone can find something that works to justify whatever it is he or she is looking to justify. It works especially well for justifying war and oppression, but there's plenty to pick from if you're willing to creatively apply lessons from the many stories found in it.

But this isn't how the Bible works. As I discovered during the many moments of reflection resulting from my spiritual midlife crisis, when we try to force the Bible to work this way, we end up stuck in a false religion that doesn't have anything to do with being like Jesus. I realized that if I truly wanted to rebuild a faith that was soundly Jesus-centered, if I wanted to maintain a belief that God is love and exactly like Jesus, I was going to have to learn to see and use the Bible differently from how I saw and used it during my days as the reigning King of Bible Memorization.

To rethink the Bible, however, we must first remember that God is love and commit to remaining unafraid. I am convinced that it is so often our fear of God, and the elevation of Scripture to the fourth member of the Trinity + 1, that prevents us from seeing the Bible in its full beauty. Viewing the Bible as being on equal footing with God subtly whispers in our ear that handling the Bible wrong or critically would be the same as handling God wrong or critically, and doing *that* could bring down his wrath. So, we just put the blankets back over our heads and pretend we didn't see and pretend we don't know what secretly we already know.

The Bible is a beautiful, divinely inspired story of God revealing himself to humanity. It is a story of people who, in ancient times, saw God as the enemy Puppy Slayer and who needed the blood of goats and rams to keep him from being overcome with anger and rage—and that makes sense, because that's what most Bronze Age goat herders thought God was like. Yet, in due time God promises that he will reveal himself, and eventually he dons flesh so that he finally reveals to the world his true nature and character. When this happens, everyone who sees God is invited to rethink everything he or she ever believed about God.

God took on human form in Jesus.

Jesus spoke.

What Jesus spoke is the Word of God.

Everything else is just a climactic buildup to that pivotal moment in human history. But to see all that, you'll have to stay committed to being unafraid.

4.

DISCOVERING YOU'RE MORE THAN JUST A SINNER

A fear-based faith distorts a lot of things, but what it distorts the most is the reflection we see in the mirror. Fear has a way of reflecting ugliness and distorted realities—lies with the appearance of truth—and gives us the false impression that fear tells the truth while concealing the reality that *fear is a liar.* It may be a *good* liar because it mixes fact with fiction, but it's a liar nonetheless. The reflections of fear must never be trusted, no matter how many nuggets of truth may be mixed in those ugly waters.

When we see God through a fear-based lens, we end up with an inaccurate view of ourselves. Like children who adopt negative lies about themselves from abusive parents—believing deep down that something is so horribly wrong with them that the parents' actions were justified—when we believe in the Puppy-Killing God found in the earliest sections of the Old Testament instead of God incarnate in Jesus in the Gospel accounts, it's quite natural to eventually believe that something is so broken and depraved about us that God's wrath, as manifest by setting us ablaze for all of eternity, must somehow be justified.

In the Gospels Jesus commanded his followers to "love your neighbor as yourself." While we often focus on the neighbor part, we forget that the "as yourself" portion means to have self-love in addition to love for God and others. However, it is nearly impossible to obey the command of Christ to love ourselves while living out a fear-based faith that begins with an angry God. If we are so worthless, so depraved, so fill-in-the-blank that we deserve to be set on fire like a victim in an ISIS execution video, it would be completely reasonable and expected that we would secretly grow to doubt whether anything inside of us was worth loving at all.

For many of us, a midlife crisis is born from identity issues that go unresolved for so long that our world has a mini-implosion. It is as if part of the human condition is the ability to get so twisted up with mixed or negative messages that we forget who we are deep at our core, why we exist, or where our lives are headed. In many cases—including mine—it's not simply that we *forget* who we are, but that we were never accurately *told* who we can be, which is a hallmark of fear-based faith. Growing up in fear-based faith, we're fed a potent mix of both the presence of damaging messages and the absence of affirming messages. The ultimate result of internalizing this distorted reflection we see in faith's fear-based mirror is a crash-and-burn moment later in life—if we don't face these things head on.

As I spent time processing the many issues that made up my midlife crisis, I grew to realize that this had been brewing since my earliest days of living and discovering myself. I think I had realized this a long time ago, but it was too painful for me to visit. The messages we received or didn't receive growing up are wounds and lies that run deep and can be difficult to untangle. For many of us, the relatively common lingering issues from childhood messages are exacerbated by a more powerful force that makes these things even more difficult to navigate well: God.

Most people, religious or not, have lingering childhood issues that rear their ugly heads in adult life. Yet for those of us who were raised in a fear-based religious tradition, these negative messages become more than what we think about ourselves and what we think others think about us: they become what we think *God* thinks about us.

And let's be honest: what God thinks about us should carry some heavy weight. That's great news for those people who grew up constantly being told how showered in God's love they were, but for those of us who grew up in fundamentalism or even conservative evangelicalism, we learned some things about ourselves that weren't just untrue but were horribly damaging to what became our adult identities. The mirror we were given to look at ourselves in was broken, and broken mirrors lead to broken thinking in one of life's most important areas: what we think about *ourselves*.

The net result of a fear-based faith isn't love as Jesus commands, but self-hatred and self-loathing. But here's the good news: once we repent of our fear of God, once we grow to see Jesus—and only Jesus—as being the Word of God, our journey will quite naturally lead us to progressively see ourselves more accurately when we look in the mirror.

Rejecting the Idea That I Am Bad

I don't think I fully realized the power of this distorted mirror until one fateful Sunday morning during worship at church.

Normally, I really connect with passionate worship. Over the years, it's one of the things that has kept me involved with an evangelical tradition instead of moving to a mainline tradition. Worship music has always been one of those ways I feel connected to God, and it often leaves me in tears as I let myself flow into the music and words each Sunday morning.

Until it hit me that morning as we sang the words from Hillsong United's "Forever Reign," "You are good, you are good, *there is nothing good in me.*"[1]

I loved that song, I loved the tune, I loved singing it—until that morning when all of a sudden I had this ginormous awareness of the message I was sending myself: "there is *nothing* good in me." I looked at the words, blown away that I had never noticed this before. I had stood in church hundreds of times, placed my hands in the air, and sung "there is nothing good in me." But this time was different—this time, something clicked inside me and I couldn't say those words. Instead, I just shook my head while muttering under my breath, *"Oh, #@%! that! I refuse to believe this anymore."*

I'll be forever grateful for the realization I had as I cussed in church that morning. The self-loathing and self-shaming that were a core part of the Christian religion I had known for most of my life had led me to a set of beliefs about myself that made it possible for me to sing that song, and sing all of it. In that moment, however, I realized that while it was certainly important to identify the fear-based things I no longer believed about God, about the Bible, or about a host of other issues, it was also critical that I let the next and oh-so-critical domino fall by identifying the things I no longer believed about *me*.

I don't believe that the people who influenced my thinking intended to send me the messages they did, but my midlife crisis helped me begin to see that the religion I had grown up with had led me to believe at least three things that were killing my faith and making the rest of my life miserable: that I was bad, that I was unlovable, and that I was hopelessly broken. Reading that, you may think I grew up in a weird cult. But I didn't. It has been my experience that plain ole vanilla expressions of Christianity often invite us—and our children—to believe these lies about ourselves. These horrid messages are even in the popular songs we sing, as I realized that morning of my awakening in this area of my life.

The Power of Narrative to Shape Identity

When I did my doctoral work at Fuller Theological Seminary, I studied the role of narrative and how narrative has the power to shape identity. From ancient times to modern ones, from Western culture to Middle Eastern culture, human beings have used narrative as a powerful force to define and shape identity. All of us human beings have found ourselves dropped in the middle of a story, and a narrative that explains who we are, and what story we're in, is one of the most powerful things that affects what we believe—not just about ourselves, but about the world around us.

The Christian narrative is a powerful one, but it is often misused, misunderstood, and misexplained such that the narrative becomes powerful in all the *wrong* ways. This critical error is unintentional, but it's an oversight with huge consequences because we begin the narrative in the wrong spot, which changes the flavor of the whole story.

For many of us, the beauty of seeing what I call God's undisrupted shalom[2] in Genesis 1, and the beauty of realizing that he created each one of us and called us *good,* is either left out of the story or treated as a minor footnote—but this is how the entire narrative of the Bible begins. Instead of beginning at the beginning when everything is "good," we tend to begin explaining the Christian narrative with sin and the idea that everyone in the world is a sinner destined for hell. Simply put, the Christian narrative so many of us are taught from our earliest, most impressionable days can be summarized like this: You. Are. Bad. So freakin' bad that you don't want to know what's going to happen if God gets his hands on you.

Here's where it gets interesting. Most modern evangelists describe human beings as wonderfully created by God and having infinite worth—if they are talking about the *unborn*. Strangely, when these evangelists talk about those *outside* of their mothers' wombs, all this language of wonder and beauty gets set aside and replaced with language about sin, damnation, and hell.

Unborn? You're wonderfully and beautifully made. You have infinite worth to God, and we must protect the sanctity of your life.

Post-born? We'll, you're really cute for a time, but as soon as you're old enough to string a few sentences together, the narrative shifts from "you are wonderfully and beautifully made" to "you are a sinner, your heart is black with sin, and you have earned yourself an eternity in hell."

We need to rewrite the narrative so we talk about ourselves in the same way we talk about the unborn: we are wonderfully and beautifully made, and we have infinite worth to God, exactly as we are. Long before sin entered the narrative in which we find ourselves, we see wonder, beauty, unbroken relationships, and God's own divine image being imparted into the people he created—and it is a beautiful beginning. It is the right place to start any narrative worthy of giving us identity: that we were created after the image of God and that we are good, beautiful, complex, and wonderful. We even see God admire our wonder and beauty, and we see God initiate intimacy with us because of it, reminding us that we're worthy of love and are desired.

It is true that sin did enter the narrative, but as my friend Kurt Willems has argued, understanding sin is best done by understanding sin as whatever disrupts the beauty and wholeness that existed in the beginning of the story; sin is what *disrupts* shalom. In this way, being saved and free from sin is critical and important—because we all long for life as it was intended, for life as it was meant to be before the great disruption occurred. That's what being saved from sin looks like: we are released from the oppression and enslavement of sin so that with God's help, our individual stories can move in the direction of wholeness again.

For example, in the Gospel of John, Jesus says that in his death "the ruler of this world will be driven out" and that he, Jesus, will then "draw all people to myself" (John 12:31–32). The imagery Jesus uses here is that of liberation from oppression; he describes defeating one who oppresses and then uses a word we translate as "to draw to," but that word more specifically means "to drag off." When we put it all together, we see an image of Jesus defeating the stranglehold of sin, driving it out, and then dragging humanity in the *opposite* direction of where sin had been taking it. It's as if Jesus wants to give us a strong visual that he is changing the narrative arc of the entire human story and moving everything back to the way it was originally supposed to be.

Yes, sin is part of this narrative. But the story of God does not *begin* with sin, as we so often describe it. It does not begin with the idea that we're all sinners. It does not begin with the idea that we are all worthy of burning in hell (in fact, hell isn't even mentioned in the Old Testament *at all*).

The true story doesn't begin with the idea that we're "bad" but begins with the idea that we're fabulous—as it's says in the book of Ephesians: "For we are God's masterpiece" (Eph 2:10, NLT). This is the beginning of God's story—and it's a beginning to the story that's in serious need of being reclaimed.

Getting the beginning of this story wrong is a pillar of fear-based faith, and it has haunted me most of my life. We can be told we are sinners and that we are worthy of hell for only so long before many of us will start to adopt this as an identity, internalize it, and live in that false narrative without realizing it. Certainly I'm aware that I sin, and yes, that makes me a sinner—and I long to be free from the sin that disrupts life as it was intended to be. However, adopting a narrative that begins with us being sinners instead of being fabulously divine image-bearers silently invites us to live a life where we walk in accordance with the belief that we are not worthy of love, that we are desperately broken, and that we are worthy of being tortured in the flames of hell. (Believe that long enough and it will really screw with you.)

Of course, American Christianity does present a "solution" within the narrative that begins with our central identity being that of sinners headed for hell, but this is a case where the cure is as dangerous as the disease. The solution so many of us were taught was that God brutally punished Jesus in our place, so when God looks at us he no longer sees us but sees Jesus *instead*.

I heard it a million times growing up: now God could look at me because *he wouldn't see me at all* but would see Jesus instead. And what did that teach me? It taught me that I was not worthy of being seen, I was not worthy of being loved, and my only solution was hiding behind someone who had taken a sound beating for me—who in fact had *died* for me. If I cowered low enough, God wouldn't see my little feet sticking out from behind Big Brother

Jesus, and Jesus would be the only one to get hit with the belt when his dad flew into a rage and tried to get at me.

We need to relearn God's image of us. One of the most beautiful examples of how this story began, and should begin, is the intimacy that existed between God and humanity in the garden—but intimacy cannot exist when one person in a relationship feels like the only way to keep the relationship intact is to hide his or her true self. In this way, the cure that some Christian preachers present is as toxic as the problem it tries to solve—for all their talk of a "personal relationship with God," it's not much of a personal relationship at all if one person feels he or she can't *even be seen* for who he or she truly is.

The first time we see this dynamic play out is right in the garden narrative. The moment Adam and Eve realize they're naked, it's as if they instantly have an awareness of self and begin to feel as if they cannot be seen for who they truly are in that moment. There is something about seeing our full and true selves that prompts us to run from others, which is precisely why I think so many people resist the hard work of developing self-awareness. It can be scary to see ourselves "naked," in nearly every sense of the word, and even more frightening to let someone else see us that way. In the case of Adam and Eve, they see their full selves and instantly pull away from God, choosing self-isolation instead of intimacy.

The first lie they believed about God was that he would purposely withhold something good from them. The second lie they believed about God was that he didn't want to see them in their full, beautiful, and complex nakedness.

And today, we believe those lies, too.

Although Adam and Eve chose to withdraw from intimacy and hide their full selves from God, God still pursued them. Seeing them in their full and imperfect complexity didn't weird God out at all; it didn't make him pull away. It's as if God wanted to send all of humanity a message that all those things that we try to hide, all the places inside of us that we don't think should ever be seen, are all things that God delights in—because he's not after perfection, he's after *intimacy in the midst of imperfection.* God isn't like a lover who loves us despite our stretch marks, despite our acne, or despite those old childhood wounds that always seem to resurface at just the "right" time. Instead, God is like a lover who truly delights in seeing all of those things we try to hide—because being allowed to see those vulnerable moments and places is the height of intimacy and the greatest gift a lover can receive.

Loving someone enough to let that person see you in all your beauty and imperfections is actually a gift that is *greater* than perfection.

Loved *Because of* Who We Are Rather Than *Despite* Who We Are

When we get our identities from the twisted version of God's narrative that starts with sin instead of goodness, we are invited into a personal narrative where, at best, we begin to view ourselves as lovable *despite who we are* instead of *because of who we are.* When we feel loved because of who we are, we claim God's love; when we feel loved despite who we are, we claim that God is able to love us only because his kid is shielding us from him, and that without that, God would be content to toss us into a lake of fire. The net result of believing this fear-based narrative that tells us we are lovable despite who we are instead of because of it is that we grow to believe we're not lovable at all. At least, that's what I spent most of my life subconsciously believing about myself.

If we get the order of the narrative right, however, we can walk through life with confidence, not self-doubt; with a sense of self-worth, not a sense of self-disgust; and with a sense of feeling loved, not with a longing for love. I believe that God longs for us to experience this, to live like this, and to bask in this. I also believe he wants us to remember what he wishes Adam and Eve had instinctively known, but didn't: we don't have to hide our true selves from him, because he's not after perfection but *intimacy*. He's not waiting for some perfected version of us; he's not disgusted by those parts of us that we'd rather keep clothed. Instead, he simply longs for us to give him the gift of allowing him to see us transparently so that he can have the opportunity to show us that he loves us completely.

Discovering a New Identity and a New Purpose: Shalom

I believe that one of the most important things we can do for ourselves is to reject the lie that we are so blackened with sin that God cannot stand to look at us. It's also true that moving beyond a fear-based faith naturally leads to the beautiful new realization that you and I are both worthy and deserving of the deepest love—not just from God, but from others as well. However, I'll admit that sin is a reality in God's narrative and that it cannot be ignored. Rejecting the narrative of my youth didn't mean that I all of a sudden believed we are perfect or that I was no longer aware of the parts of me that are in fact beat up or broken and in need of healing and restoration. Instead, I had to look again at God's narrative and find a way to make sense of everything—and it had to be a way of viewing the narrative that would leave me believing I was worthy of being loved while also giving a proper account to the reality of sin in the world, and even in me.

For me, this process happened in seminary when I wrote my doctoral dissertation, which focused, among other topics, on developing a personal theology of *shalom* that could be used in the field of trauma recovery. This process put together for the first time the pieces left over from my dissembled faith. As I dug deep into the theology of *shalom*, I was returned to the beginning of God's story, which is exactly where I needed be. Sometimes, going back to the beginning of a story and starting over is the best thing to do.

We can't understand God until we understand the undivided essence of God, which is love. God is pure love—he's not love plus something we need to fear, but simply love, and love alone. As I said earlier, God is love, period. Thus, when the opening verses of Genesis say that we were created in the image and likeness of God, it is helpful to remember that this means we are actually created in the image and likeness of *love*.

We were created *by* love.

We were created to *receive* love.

We were created to *reflect* love.

Our entire purpose for existing is *love*.

You and I, at our core, have love as a starting point, because we were created in the image of God in order to grow and blossom in a divine process of becoming more and more like God—and the core of who God is, and what God does, is *love*.

I like how Thomas Jay Oord puts it: " 'God is love' means love is the necessary expression of God's timeless nature. God relentlessly expresses love . . . God *must* love. To put it as a double negative: God cannot not love . . . God could no more stop loving than stop existing."[3]

Just as any doctrine of God that does not begin with love as the core and immutable essence of God's nature and character would be distorted, any version of who you are or who I am that does not begin with the reality that we were created in the image of love, in order to receive and reflect love, is grossly distorted as well. God is love, and he could never stop loving. We were created in the image of God, and as his image-bearers, we too are called to never stop loving and *being* loved.

Love is where we begin God's story—and love is where we begin ours.

We then see this perfect, untainted love expressed in the beautiful creation poem of Genesis 1 where all the unbroken elements of God's shalom existed in perfection—we see life as it was intended to be, in perfect love. Humanity had an unbroken relationship with God, an unbroken relationship with each other, an unbroken relationship with creation; their physical needs were cared for, their emotional needs were cared for, they had a present purpose for living, and they had a future goal to look forward to. Those elements, in unbroken form, make up the way life was originally intended to be.[4] When you put all of these categories together, you have what I call "undisrupted shalom."

Of course, sin *does* enter the creation story, and God's shalom is grandly disrupted. Our relationships—with God and with each other, and even with the world and environment around us—are broken in every direction. But let us get this clear: the story does not start with sin. Nor does sin ever become the core identity of what it means to be human. Nothing can change the core identity of who God is and who we are: we were created by love, created in the image of love, and created for the purpose of receiving and reflecting love. The only thing that changed in the story was the context of the setting—it went from peace and perfection to disrupted and broken.

Using this relearned understanding of who we are and our purpose on earth reframes everything. Under this light, we can see that sin is simply anything that disrupts the way life is intended to be. Sometimes we are the ones who do the disrupting; sometimes it's done to us. But never does sin become part of our identity. We are created in the image and likeness of love, and nothing can destroy that.

Of course, God longs for us to be free from that force as well, which is why the rest of God's narrative is all about God's grand plan to free us, or as Jesus put it, to ransom us. God's entire movement throughout history can then be reframed as the actions he takes to free us from anything that gets in the way of our ability to perfectly receive love, and to perfectly give love.

But let us be clear on another point: in this story we are not God's enemies. We are God's image-bearers and the most precious thing he created. We are not sin but are oppressed by the force of sin. We need saving but not from God or even ourselves—we need saving from all of those many things that interfere with our ability to perfectly reflect and receive love.

This was God's plan and desire all along: for us to realize that we were created by love, in the image and likeness of love, so that we might perfectly reflect love and perfectly receive love.

And it is *still* God's plan—and this is what the entire narrative of God is about!

Revisiting God's narrative and getting it right the second or third time around is a powerful step toward rethinking the twisted narratives about God *and* about ourselves. When we realize that our deepest identity is love, and our deepest purpose is to give and receive love, we develop an unquenchable desire to fulfill our purpose—and to shed and resist anything that might get in the way of that.

Learning to Recognize Our Distorted Lenses Is a Constant Process

We spend so much time thinking about God. We spend time thinking about theology. We spend time thinking about so many things—but what we miss is the reality that we cannot rethink God without also rethinking ourselves. We need to learn how to go a step beyond simply thinking about God and make sure that we are allowing what we think about God to change and shape what we think about *ourselves*. It is far easier to change our minds about who we think God is than to change our minds about who we are. For example, as many of us well know, it is easier to believe that God is love and completely loving than it is to actually embrace the belief that we are lovable.

I love having my beliefs expanded and challenged. In many ways I have grown even to love the process in which that occurs. During my Christian journey, the many years I spent in seminary, and certainly much of the processing I did during the specific life chapter I write about in this book, I found myself repeatedly rethinking everything. However, this life chapter was unique because I finally realized a critical component of theology that I had missed for years and years: if what we believe about God doesn't invite us to rethink what we believe about ourselves, we're not really done rethinking yet. In other words, if we are the image-bearers of God, what we believe about God naturally leads us to what we believe about ourselves. A theology of God and a theology of self cannot be separated.

In this way, I think many people are missing a critical component involved in a faith shift. I meet or receive messages from people every day who have gone though massive faith transformations in their lifetimes—transformations that radically altered who they believe God to be and what they believe God to be like. One of the things I have noticed over the years as I have listened to the wounds and struggles of those people is that many of them have not made the connection that *rethinking God means rethinking themselves.* Many have embraced a God who is loving, but they still struggle to do more than mentally assent to the idea that they might be lovable.

For those of us who ultimately connect these dots, such a connection often seems to come at the end of our faith transformation: we sit back one day and realize that everything we were rethinking has massive implications for our understanding of who we are. It's fantastic that so many people rethink themselves at the end of their transformations, but I can't help wishing that I had been aware of this earlier in my journey— which is precisely why I'm discussing this earlier in this book, and not later. If I had realized that internalizing good theology could be so healing, I would have found myself coming back to life much sooner in my process. Seeing God and ourselves through the right light is ever-changing, and how we choose to see God, and how we choose to see ourselves (and it is an active choice), becomes a lens through which we filter and interpret everything we see and experience around us.

The Apostle Paul mentions this in 1 Corinthians when he tells the church at Corinth, "Now we see imperfectly, like puzzling reflections in a mirror" (1 Cor 13:12, NLT). While it certainly won't be possible to ever see ourselves or God perfectly on this side of eternity, we do know the baseline of what we *should* see, and this knowledge is what we must use to combat the distorted lies we are so often told about God and about ourselves. Let me tell you a story about distorted vision—because this is something I have some unique experience with.

During my military years I was fortunate enough to get picked up as a professional military education instructor on the beautiful Pacific island of Guam. I loved my years there; it was the best job I ever had, and there was nothing better than coming home at the end of the day and snorkeling along the reef. However, about a year into my tour on Guam, I realized that I didn't like living as far inland as I did and decided to move to a condo that was within walking distance of both the ocean life and the nightlife.

After a long day of moving, I was scheduled to meet up with some of my mates at our favorite karaoke bar (a setting quite different from a karaoke bar back on the mainland, but it's the kind of thing you'd have to experience to understand). I was running late but figured I'd just move a few more boxes before walking down to the club. I was in a rush and being careless, so when I turned quickly to grab and move another box, I failed to see that a small metal pole from a beach chair was sticking out in just the right way (and by "just the right way," I mean in the worst possible way). Having misjudged the depth of how close the pole was to me, I accidentally turned into it, and the pole jabbed my eye.

At dinner parties, this is where people cringe and ask me not to finish the story. But since this is a book and I can't hear you telling me to stop, I'll finish: I had never felt such intense pain, and I immediately collapsed and went into an instant full-body sweat. Once the initial wave of pain finished going through my body and the ringing in my ears lessened, I could sense that something was way, way wrong—so I ran to the bathroom to look in a mirror to see what I had done to myself. Sparing you *those* gory details, let me just tell you this: what I saw made me collapse again, and I knew I wasn't heading for a karaoke bar—I was heading for a hospital.

What happened at the hospital was a frightening experience in its own right. I soon learned that when the pole jammed into my eye, it shaved off 80 percent of my cornea—a feat so impressive that the guy providing my initial treatment stopped for a moment, walked to the door of the exam room, and shouted into the hallway, "You gotta come see this! You probably won't ever get to see something like this again." Thanks to his grand announcement, before I knew it, a dozen people were clustered around me in the exam room oohing and aahing at what an eye looks like with the cornea hanging out and a screaming human attached to it.

All this, of course, had me panicked about my prognosis, so I directly asked, "Am I going to lose my eye?"

The guy's answer, after an hour of treating me and trying to get every person in the hospital to come look at my eye, left me in more shock than the injury itself: "I don't know," he said. "I'm just a nurse. You'll have to come back tomorrow when we have an eye doctor working." So much for military hospitals.

With that, I was sent home with a pirate patch and a bottle of pain meds to wait out what became an intensely painful healing process. Thankfully, I did not end up losing my sight, but my injury that evening did leave me with chronic eye problems, as my cornea did not perfectly reattach to the rest of my eye, and where it did, I was left with scarring. This scarring now often creates double vision in that eye, especially at night.

Having distorted vision in one eye has certainly been discouraging, but it's one of those things you get used to and then forget about. I had accepted this one option for literally viewing the world. This was the case for me until one fateful visit to the eye doctor when the doctor did two things differently. First, he took a photo of the scar on my eye, and second, instead of simply asking me to read a line of letters on the opposite wall, he had me read them while peering through a small pinhole that he placed over my eye. Looking through the small pinhole I found myself shocked to see that, for the first time in as long as I could remember, I was able to see perfectly without a hint of double vision.

As the doctor described it to me, the pinhole acted as a kind of filter that blocked out all of the things that were distorting my vision and helped me see things as they truly are. Unfortunately, I can't walk around looking at everything through a pinhole, but that experience did at least remind me how we often see the reality around us as distorted—and it reminded me that often it takes an external filter to help us sift out what is true and what only *appears* to be true because we view it through our many different distorted lenses. It also taught me that I was capable of growing and expanding my lens of the world, even later in my life when I thought I would forever fail at reading the letters on the opposite wall.

In the same way, when we see the world through one unchanging lens, we distort our reality and forget that we're looking through a lens in the first place. These lenses completely bend and shape our realities; they determine how we assign meaning to our life's events; and they most certainly shape how we view ourselves. But they are changeable, and that's where the growth happens. While the idea of having such a lens is neither positive nor negative, the reality is that it is highly likely that your lenses—and mine—are actually rooted in untrue messages we have been taught about ourselves. It's also true that it's impossible to unbelieve these lies until we name them and look directly at the imperfections on our lenses—just as I did that day in the eye doctor's office as he showed me a large digital image of the scar across my cornea.

Naming the lens is a big step toward being able to change and grow. Looking at the image of the scar across my cornea was powerful for me because I was finally able to look directly at the culprit of my vision issues. It was an even more powerful moment when I decided I was going to name and identify the distorted lenses that shaped how I viewed myself, because if we're going to identify the things we no longer believe about God anymore, but never get around to naming the things we don't believe about ourselves, the entire process of growth and enlightenment is stunted.

For me, that process needed to begin by reminding myself of the correct lens through which to view myself and life: God loves me, not *despite* who I am, but *because of* who I am. Any message about myself that even remotely disagreed or hindered that ultimate reality was a distorted lens that I knew needed to be named and no longer believed.

This realization meant that I had to do the hard work of naming those lies about myself that I was going to choose to stop believing. My life story is clothed in feelings of rejection. From the suicide of my grandfather when I was seventeen years old to failed marriages (yes, plural), and to other life experiences where meaning became distorted for me, I've walked away from all of those experiences with messages about myself that are simply untrue even though they have felt *very* true. I have many years of experience deeply internalizing feelings of inadequacy, of not being good enough, of not being loved or valued; believing that my heart is not worthy of being seen in its true form; and generally feeling completely insignificant. Some of those lies began with what I was taught about God, and some were born out of life's heartache; but all of them blended together to be the lenses through which I would spend so much of my life looking at myself and functionally living as if I agreed with what I saw. Those lenses held an oppressive power over me—until I had the courage to say their names out loud.

Unspoken lies tend to immediately lose their power once we choose to be unafraid and speak them out loud; they have power over us only until we finally decide to directly confront them. If there's one thing you take away from this book, I pray it is this: saying out loud and naming what you don't believe anymore breaks the power that fear holds over you. When you do this, you can grow and reshape your lenses, and ultimately yourself and your image of God.

Although the process of rethinking ourselves and unbelieving those things that are not true is an ongoing, lifelong process, for me a major leap was actually writing down all of the lies I had believed about myself. I did this by listing words—words that meant something to me, words that had power over me, words that defined and oppressed me. I wrote down all the main words that had ever caused me to forget my real, true identity and purpose. When I was done writing them down, I looked at each one of them as if they were some monster from my emotional closet that I had hidden from but never looked in the eyes and confronted. After facing off with each one of them, I said their names out loud:

Unlovable.

Bad.

Insignificant.

Ugly.

Disgusting.

Forgettable.

Needy.

Weak.

Hated.

Broken.

Depraved.

After saying them out loud multiple times—letting each one know that I was on to what it was doing to me—I said what is one of the most powerful sentences I ever spoke on my spiritual journey: *"I don't believe that about me anymore."*

Few things shape us as much as the stories we believe we find ourselves in. For far too many years of my life, I had derived my identity from a narrative that told me I was so broken and so bad that I was not worthy of even being seen. My only hope was to hide behind the one who was worthy—Jesus. This basic fear-based narrative I had been taught *seemed* to be confirmed by my own traumatic life experiences—experiences that played right into a core belief that I was broken, worthy of rejection, and unlovable.

This is perhaps the reason I will be most eternally grateful for having a midlife crisis: it forced me to rethink everything, and rethinking everything would not be complete without *rethinking me.* By fully embracing this process, I came to see that I had gotten God's narrative completely wrong—or at least, I had left off the critical beginning that changes the entire narrative: I was made by love, in the image of love, so that I could receive and reflect love. Anything other than this core reality was simply a scar on my emotional cornea that totally distorted what was true and real about me.

Getting our lenses fixed and allowing ourselves to continually grow and heal makes all the difference in the world. Yes, the narrative always begins with God, but what we think about God has a direct correlation to what we think about ourselves. These two are inseparable and make theology something that can heal, or can wound—because when our theology in this area gets mixed with life experiences, we develop powerful lenses that have the ability to both heal and wound. Instead of filtering everything we see and our experiences in life through our lenses of rejection and negative messages we have been taught about ourselves, maybe God is inviting us to begin moving all the things we're told about ourselves through a filter that begins with the ultimate reality: God is love.

We were created by love and in the image of love.

We were created to receive and reflect love.

We have unsurpassable worth ascribed to us by God—and nothing can take that away.

The net result of a correct filter of self is the realization that God loves us not *despite* who we are, but *because* of who we are.

Anything else? Any other message about God or ourselves? Well, anything else is something that we should write out on a piece of paper, stare in the face, and say, "I don't believe that anymore."

5.

ENDING THE END TIMES NARRATIVE

The stories we believe matter. Just as we need to rethink the beginning of the story of our relationship with God, we need to rethink our fear-based view of how this story is going to end.

While I was in the middle part of my spiritual crisis—sifting through my spiritual woes, beginning with relinquishing my fears toward God; rethinking my upbringing of trying to use the Bible like it was a Swiss Army knife; and learning that love is the filter that needs to filter my view of everything—I found myself repeatedly wanting to avoid and escape the whole exhausting process. When one has spent a lifetime reading from a very specific script, learning to read from an entirely new one can be draining and emotionally taxing—*even if you actually really like the new script.*

Having a clear image of the endgame is especially important when you're in the thick of your spiritual crisis. Inspirational posters tell us that we shouldn't miss out on the joy of the journey, and this was an especially hard message to accept when I went

through my rocky process. Nothing about going through a
spiritual midlife crisis is fun. There's no joy in waking up in the
morning and not wanting to get out of bed. There's no joy in
lying there at night, wondering whether you took the whole love
thing too far and so you're going to end up in the seventh level of
the hell you don't believe in anymore. There's no joy in watching
your friends walk away from you because you no longer hold to
whatever beliefs they thought were necessary in order to be your
friend (those pesky guns and gays again). And there's certainly no
joy in watching someone stand up and storm out of your church
because you had advocated for a higher minimum wage during
a television interview a few weeks before. (Yes, that *actually*
happened.) In the midst of all of it, I think I would have done
just about anything to avoid all of it. But I couldn't. I needed to
push through it to get to the other side. And there's an important
reason why.

Making it through the unlearning and deconstruction phase of
my spiritual journey allowed me to accept a more hopeful sense of
my future. I realized that in order to navigate the kind of implosion
many of us eventually experience within fear-based faith, I needed
to let go of my pessimism for the future and my desire to escape
or rush the process. For me, letting go of that meant I had to stop
believing that this experience in life was somehow going to
end badly. Sure, ending badly is always a possibility, but if I set out
believing that, ending badly was probably more of a sure thing
instead of just one of several potential outcomes. Even if I couldn't
see it in the moment, I just *had* to believe that it was not only
going to be okay, but that this journey was actually going to lead to
somewhere beautiful in the end.

My personal process of reimagining a hopeful narrative of
where God's story is headed obviously involved spending a lot of

time sifting through the crap I was taught about God as a kid. As I've said, part of this was realizing I had been handed a narrative to make meaning of my life, and the beginning of that narrative naturally invited feelings of self-loathing and the belief that I had to hide the essence of who I have always known myself to be. But once I realized the damaging effect of how this narrative began, I realized that the narrative problem in Christianity is much worse than what I initially thought. For the narrative not only begins with a destructive message that has unintended consequences, but *it often ends that way also.* In fact, many people believe they're living within a nightmarish story that ends very badly.

Consider in a nutshell the whole fear-based narrative Biblicists have produced and taught: God creates the universe and declares it to be good and beautiful—from the outer cosmos to the individual human. All is good until a lady in the story is enticed by a talking snake to eat the wrong fruit, at which point God condemns those previously beautiful creations to an eternity of being burned alive, with never-ending conscious torment. From this point, it gets a bit worse because God doesn't just condemn *Adam and Eve* to this torturous future but the *entire human race.* Yet, have no fear: God has a plan. God will save a handful of people by torturing his own son instead—which he does later in the story. After he has watched his son slowly suffer and die, his anger is subdued enough to invite some of his beautiful creations back into a relationship with him, but with the vast majority of people (usually those born in the wrong country) still going to a place he created called hell. In the meantime, prepare for a one-world government run buy a guy called the antichrist who will cut off your head if you don't let him give you a tattoo on the front of it. To top it all off, God is now moving the human story to a climactic moment where so many people will be slaughtered that blood will run in the streets as high as a horse's bridle when Jesus returns as an alter ego of himself (oh, but don't worry—all the Christians will magically disappear before this happens). This time, gone is the soft and loving Jesus—it's time for the world to meet the pissed-off tattooed warrior who finally gets his licks in before throwing the majority of everyone who has ever lived into a lake of fire.

But there's "good news" in this narrative: a few of the lucky chosen ones will live happily ever after with God and Jesus, who aren't so angry anymore.

This is the narrative I was taught as a kid. And I was told that it is the most wonderful story ever. I was told that this is all really, really good news. But I'm sorry, this isn't good news at all. If this narrative is really true, it's actually *horrible news* if you ask me, especially the ending.

It shouldn't have been such a shock to me that I was a pessimist—as this is a powerfully negative, fear-based narrative. If it begins negatively, and if it ends negatively, we should probably expect those caught in the middle to act negatively—and that's exactly what happened to me. As I struggled and processed my own fearfully destructive outlook on life, I realized that what we believe about God's story matters—especially what we believe about how this story is going to *end*. For me, it wasn't enough to simply go back and get the beginning of God's narrative right; I had to completely rethink where God's story was heading and how it was all going to end, too.

Growing up, I believed that God's story, and the entire created universe, was getting ready to end—we were at the "end times." Now like I said, technically, preachers claimed that this was good news, but that's simply because we believed we were going to get raptured out of the world before God opened the seal of his wrath and began smiting all of creation before destroying it with fire—sort of the way a cat likes to bat a mouse around for a while before killing and eating it. This belief about how God's story ends has an intense ability to influence the way we see our own stories in the here and now. If we are just small players situated within a pessimistic story that ends badly, what hope is there? Is it possible that this belief system is so powerful, and runs so deep, that the pessimism and doom-and-gloom can begin to permeate all other areas of our lives, killing off any sort of faith that produces beauty?

I believe it can—and does. What we believe about the future matters, and it deeply affects what we think, believe, and do today.

As I navigated my process of identifying things I no longer believed anymore, I began to see that beyond affirming that God is love and that God is exactly like Jesus, I also had developed a general pessimism and avoidance that was rooted in years of indoctrination regarding the horrible direction that God's story (and thus my story) was heading. If anything were to change, I had to take the next step and finally uproot and discard any lingering end time beliefs that choked out my optimism and hope for the future. I knew that if I were to have a Christian faith, it had to be one full of hope. It just *had* to. The negativity and pessimism were killing me.

Fruit of the Rapture

A pessimistic view of the future can make us do some crazy things. I remember Sunday, May 22, 2011; the entire weekend was full of beautiful spring weather. But although the sun was shining in New England, this day was a dark and nightmarish one for some American Christians, such as Joel and Adrienne Martinez. The Martinez family had been disciples of Harold Camping, who had predicted that the rapture—when all Christians would be removed from the earth and the seven-year Great Tribulation would begin—was to occur on Saturday evening, May 21, of that year. Except, as we all know, it didn't. While Camping's failed rapture prediction alone may not have been such a big deal to folks like the Martinez family, how they had prepared for it *was* a big deal. Joel and Adrienne had been so convinced they were leaving the planet on May 21 that they spent their life savings on rapture advertising, timing their spending so that their savings would be fully depleted on that date. They were sure they'd be in heaven on May 22 and not need any of the money.[1]

Disturbingly, this family wasn't alone. There was also Abby Haddad-Carson, who quit her job two years before May 21, 2011; stopped saving money for her children's college education; and spent her time and money warning people that Judgment Day was looming.[2] Robert Fitzpatrick, a retiree who bought into the rapture prediction (literally), spent more than $140,000 to help spread the word that the rapture was around the corner. Sadly, the only thing his life savings bought him was an uncomfortable moment on May 21, standing in the middle of Times Square and telling the crowd, "I see that we're still here. . . . I don't understand why nothing has happened."[3]

While some people, such as the Martinez family and Fitzpatrick, believed they would be leaving this world for heaven on that date, others believed the opposing end of their rapture message—that they would be left behind on earth to face the Great Tribulation set to begin on May 22. One such tragic case of an individual who thought she'd be left behind was Lyn Benedetto. She tried to spare herself and her children from the horrors that would unfold during those seven years of hell on earth before it was upon them. On the predicted

Judgment Day of May 21 she slit her throat with a box cutter, but only after slitting the throats of her eleven- and fourteen-year-old daughters (they all three survived).[4] I don't even need to continue writing into the next paragraph for you to begin picking up what I'm laying down: pessimistic eschatology (that is, what we believe about the end of the story) has an amazing power to produce some really, really horrible fruit.

Although the majority of American Christians laughed off Camping's prediction that the rapture would occur on May 21, 2011, and bring on the Great Tribulation, a shocking number of them—particularly the majority of evangelicals—actually share Camping's view of the future; it differs only in its timing.

This view of the future stems from a theological system called "dispensationalism," and though many people may not recognize the name for it, far too many of us grow up being taught at least some of the more fear-based aspects of it. In its basic form, dispensationalism is a grid-work applied to the Bible, history, and the future that drastically affects how we view and interpret these things. Dispensationalism categorizes history and the future into periods of time (called, you guessed it, "dispensations"). On the surface, using categories to make meaning of history or the future isn't necessarily a bad thing, but dispensationalism has a particular poison tucked into it, which has for the better part of the past century been dominant: the pessimistic view that the world is getting progressively worse and that we can't do anything to stop it. After the rapture, the Great Tribulation will be unleashed on earth before a fiery end to everything around us. Throw in that one-world government, the antichrist, and the mark of the beast, and you have the view of the future that Camping and many evangelicals share today—and it's the view of the future that so many of us, myself included, grew up believing.

Things Weren't Always This Darn Depressing

During my years at Gordon-Conwell Theological Seminary, I
had the wonderful opportunity to study a few different areas of
Christian history under the tremendous guidance of respected
Church historian Garth Rosell. One of the classes I took with Dr.
Rosell was on Christian history in the United States. It sounded
interesting in the class catalogue, but the format of the class
turned out to be initially disappointing. Instead of listening
to Rosell lecture (which was what I was hoping for, as he had a
radio voice combined with a unique way of making history more
interesting), the class would, as a whole, read through about
one hundred books over the semester that covered the gamut of
Christianity in the United States from the country's inception to
the present day. Each student was assigned various books to read
and would summarize their books for the rest of the class—each
week traversing through another era of U.S. Christian history. I
decided to remain in the class after being assigned John Adams's
biography (a book I was interested in reading), but I quickly
came to regret my decision when we were assigned the next
round of books.

   I remember clearly the day I was assigned that stupid book.
Everyone else in the class got really cool titles to read; but my book,
which had one of those transparent, plastic library book covers
that had yellowed with the years, *looked* boring from the second I
took it off the self. To make matters worse, at this time I was going
through what felt like a transition out of evangelical Christianity,
and the name of the book was *Discovering an Evangelical Heritage*,
by Donald W. Dayton. Discovering an evangelical *anything* was
pretty much the last thing on my to-do list. I begrudgingly checked

the book out—but it sat in my backpack until two days before I was supposed to present it to the class.

The day I picked it up to read it, I was half tempted to just review the table of contents and wing my presentation—I've always been good on my feet that way. However, a voice of integrity in my ear said that I should at least skim it, so I sat down and began reading its faded pages. I didn't expect to experience what happened, but within a few pages I was *absolutely hooked* and couldn't put the book down. It was as if I were being introduced to the kind of Christianity I had longed for—not by an argument of what *could be,* but rather by opening my eyes to what *had already been.*

In a profound moment of clarity and inspiration I saw that evangelicalism *then* was strikingly different from evangelicalism *now.* As that annoying plastic book cover crinkled with each page I turned, I was introduced to a nineteenth-century evangelicalism that wasn't focused on escaping the world, but *transforming* it. Seriously—the early evangelicals in the United States were badasses for Jesus. These were the fearless people like Elijah Lovejoy, who kept buying printing presses to mass produce antislavery materials, even though mobs destroyed the press each time he got a new one (and eventually shot and killed him). Or people like Theodore Weld, who co-wrote (along with his wife and her sister) the 1839 book *American Slavery As It Is*, which was essentially a documentary before documentaries were around and was so powerful that it ignited antislavery outrage throughout the Northern states. From the establishment of the American Red Cross to antipoverty initiatives by the Salvation Army, orphan care, prison reform, and nearly anything else you could imagine, early evangelicals in the United States were deeply and self-sacrificially invested in the long-term betterment of society. Even hellfire preachers were in on this early social justice game, as revivalists such as Charles Finney went around the country preaching not simply the need for conversion, but also the need for individuals to become what he called "socially useful."

The optimistic worldview of these early American evangelicals led them to accomplish some amazing things—things that still affect us positively today. The core reason they were so optimistic and dedicated to making long-term investments in society is because these early evangelicals held to a completely different view of the end of the world than what today's evangelicals typically learn when they are young. You see, the fear-based, escapist narrative that says Christians will be airlifted off the planet before seven years of chaos and destruction begin *didn't exist* in the minds of these earlier movers and shakers. When they viewed the future, they were unafraid.

Instead of a fear-based view of the future that saw the world as getting progressively *worse,* they held to a view of the end times which believed that the world is getting progressively *better*—that the global church will successfully grow, society will improve, and the church will help the world move toward peace, eventually ending with the return of Jesus. Because these early evangelicals were so unafraid as they viewed the future, they became some of the most inspirational people in U.S. history. They were Christians who believed their job was to make the world a better place, and they were driven by the deep-seated belief that *nothing* had the power to stop them. Peering at them through the eyes of history, I discovered a beautiful Christian worldview that I hardly dared to dream of as a child of dispensationalism.

These Christians continued their optimistic march toward progress until Christianity was influenced by a man who was perhaps the biggest dream-crusher in all of Christian history: a preacher from England named John Nelson Darby.

Hope Rebuked

Few individuals have screwed up the world as much as John Nelson Darby (1800–1882) has. That may sound harsh, but I promise you, it's true. If I were to compare Darby to someone in your circle of friends, he'd be that person who shows up at a party where everyone is happy and having a good time but before long manages to get everyone to sit in the living room and complain about how much their jobs suck. An obscure lawyer turned preacher in England (though he was theologically uneducated),[5] Darby began selling a vision of the future that was the exact opposite of the dominant position of his time. Instead of the focus on forward progress, the dedication to continually making the world a better place, and the belief that the church established by Christ would be successful in a world that would get increasingly *better* until his return, Darby taught that the world was going to hell in a handbasket and actively rebuked the hopes of his generation. In a lecture he gave in Geneva in 1840 he stated:

> What we are about to consider will tend to show that, instead of permitting ourselves to hope for a continued progress of good, we must expect a progress of evil; and that the hope of the earth being filled with the knowledge of the Lord before the exercise of His judgment, and the consummation of this judgment on the earth, is delusive. We are to expect evil, until it becomes so flagrant that it will be necessary for the Lord to judge it.[6]

Darby became known as the father of dispensationalism, and his theology presented the world with a new narrative through which to view the future—one that was hopelessly fear-based at the core. Darby either invented or popularized nearly everything we see in the modern end times movement—from the idea of a secret rapture of a church; and the distinction between the church and Israel, which has led American Christians to actively support apartheid and the genocide of the Palestinian people, including fellow Christians; to the progress toward evil. In hindsight, we see that concepts Darby invented, such as the rapture, are so ingrained in Christian culture today that the majority of folks do not even realize that these *new concepts* are not part of the Christian religion. Between convincing people that the world was hopelessly on the decline toward destruction and inventing the idea that one day Christians would be zapped out of here, Darby was to the nineteenth century what someone who invents a computer virus in order to sell you a pop-up blocker is to our century.

At first, Darby's weird teachings didn't catch on in the United States, but eventually it took less than a generation for them to spread like dandelion seeds in the wind and take root. Churches and Bible schools cropped up all across the country dedicated not to the Christian message as it always had been, but to teaching young American Christians this new, fear-based end times fanaticism that has become the hallmark of dispensationalism. Combine this wildfire spread of churches and Bible schools with two world wars (events that seemed to prove Darby right), and Americanized Christianity was hooked on the drug of fear.

Finally, perhaps one of the most long-term and deep cultural agents of influence for this worldview came with the publication of the Scofield Reference Bible in 1909 (revised in 1917). The Scofield Reference Bible included Darby's pessimistic ideas about the future alongside the biblical text, leading impressionable Bible readers to assign them the same authority as Scripture itself. With that, what began as some crazy ideas by an untrained British preacher became central to Americanized Christianity as Darby's teachings were elevated to the level of Holy Scripture and mass produced for public consumption across the fruited plain.

Darby's fear-based view of the future eventually won the day over the Christian view of optimism and hope and became the dominant "Christian" position in evangelical America. Once some Christians discovered that this unorthodox way of interpreting Scripture and viewing the future was a fast-track to riches and power, there was no looking back. The American values of commercialization and profit quickly took over and became the new driving forces behind our fear-based view of the future—bringing us things like the creepy movie *A Thief in the Night* (1972) (which birthed the tradition of children worrying they'd wake up and find themselves left behind and parentless after the rapture), the book and movie *The Late, Great Planet Earth* (book, 1970; movie, 1976), the book *88 Reasons Why the Rapture Will Be in 1988*, the Left Behind series of novels (1995–2007), the apocalyptic blood-moon prophecy promoted in the book *Four Blood Moons* (2013), and ultimately an entire new genre of literature. Just looking at the Left Behind series we see a brand that has included fifty-eight million books in print with more than twenty million in spin-offs and an annual sustained revenue of $100 million.[7] And that's just *one* series within a much larger genre! The *New York Times* bestseller *Four Blood Moons* by John Hagee has sold millions of copies and certainly padded Hagee's personal net worth of $5 million.[8] He'll undoubtedly continue raking in the dough well after history shows that he was just another false prophet who got rich incorrectly predicting the future.

John Nelson Darby's ideas have become so profitable for the Christian publishing industry (end times books are the Christian

version of porn) that the dominant power holders have no reason
to reject this false, fear-based faith, as the entire end times genre
is making many people quite rich and powerful. The basic game
flows something like this: persuade the masses that the world is
going to hell in a handbasket, tell them that your books will predict
the future and equip them for navigating the disasters ahead,
and get as many of them into your political party as possible.
Rinse, lather, repeat, and you'll be both wealthy and powerful.
(For example, Tim Lahaye was not simply the coauthor of the Left
Behind series; he also sat on the Board of Directors of the Moral
Majority. Furthermore, some significant foreign policy positions
of both the Republican and Democratic parties actually stem from
dispensationalism's unique view of Israel.) As with most things
in American culture, we go big or we go home, and with doom-
and-gloom end times theology, we've gone *big*. Yet the average
Christian doesn't realize that this twisted worldview is less than
two hundred years old. We eat it because it's what we've always
been fed, not because it's actually what's most nourishing—or true.

The result? Darby's narrative of fear with the promise of
escape has, for the last generation or so, invited Christians to
focus on "winning souls" before our imminent escape from the
world, instead of inviting us to become agents of change and
reconciliation determined to make the world the kind of place
Jesus would be proud to return home to. Sadly, far too many of us
have accepted Jesus's invitation and spend our time waiting for the
train to come into the station instead of working to build the track
it will ride on—and the world has suffered the results.

What's worse is that this fear of the future and desire to escape
has spread like cancer, no longer being limited merely to our
eschatology. In many ways, it has covered much of Christianity
in a toxic blanket of fear, pessimism, and negativity. As if getting

the beginning of God's story wrong weren't bad enough—inviting us to live as if we're either unlovable or loved despite who we are instead of because if it—getting the ending of the story wrong seals us into a narrative that kills. And this is why the Americanized end times nonsense is so destructive: if we believe the story is going to end badly, we will most likely *start acting in ways that invite that ending.* We invite that ending for the world, and we invite that kind of ending for our own personal narratives—which is precisely why I realized I needed to dig deep and remove this root of programmed fear of the future if I were to emerge from my faith transition a healthy person with a bright outlook on the world around me.

What We Believe About the Future Actually Matters

Throughout history Christians have identified issues that are core and central to being a Christian, as well as areas of belief that are considered "disputable matters" where Christians can exercise charitable disagreement. For far too long what we believe about the future has been considered one of those issues that is completely disputable, as if the consequences of our belief in this area are somehow harmless. For those of us who long to move beyond a fear-based faith, however, this cannot be seen as disputable—because what we believe about the future *actually matters* in the here and now, because it influences *what we do* in the here and now.

I can think of no other issue that affects our behavior in the here and now more than how we *think* this story is going to end; my view of the direction of this narrative has certainly influenced me since my childhood. I grew up believing that the world was headed to hell in a handbasket and that shit was about to get real at any moment. It was drilled into my head over and over that the rapture was so close it could happen even tomorrow. Of course, me being fear-based me, I obsessed over that fact.

My obsession with the timing of the rapture started in the eighth grade and lasted a few years. I suppose all kids at that age have something they get obsessive about. For some of my friends, all they could think about was baseball cards. Other friends seemed to care only about music. Me? Well, I spent my days obsessing over whether or not the rapture was going to happen before I got to see a pair of real-life boobs.

This is actually 100 percent true and why I would get so discouraged and frustrated when preachers taught that the end times were upon us. I was convinced that the rapture was coming and I was going to be one of the millions of hormonally dominated teenagers whom God was going to cheat out of having sex or even getting a glimpse of second base. I was sure this was to be my lot in life: the experience would finally arrive, I'd undo the first few buttons, I'd embrace the right of passage of struggling to figure out the closures of a bra . . . and then before I finished I'd be magically whisked through the roof and spend eternity in heaven where I was taught there will be no sex at all. As a child of the teachings of dispensationalism, *that's* what I worried about.

This principle that our view of the future drives current behavior plays out for all of us, and a fear-based view of eschatology leads to, ironically, either overtly or passively destructive behavior in the here and now. As disgraced Calvinist pastor Mark Driscoll once said at an evangelical conference: "I know who made the environment and he's coming back and going to burn it all up. So yes, I drive an SUV."[9]

Tragically, Driscoll's somewhat tongue-and-cheek, but also

totally serious, statement points to the deeper reality when it comes to doom-and-gloom end times theology. Let's think about it for a second: If the world is going to be destroyed, if Armageddon is inevitable, if life on earth is going to get progressively worse, and all Christians are going to experience an imminent departure from it, why invest ourselves in the opposite side of a losing battle? Why bother making multigenerational investments into reforming broken social systems? Why work to transform society into a more beautiful expression of what it is not, but what it could be? Why worry about endangered species, oil spills, and greenhouse gasses if (a) we're leaving soon and (b) Jesus is just going to destroy the world anyway? Why bother doing any of it? The invitation to escape is powerful—it's why so many people fall prey to the addiction of drugs and alcohol. Yet, as followers of the way of Jesus, our invitation is not to escape to heaven, but to make heaven a reality wherever we are in the present moment. We're invited not to escape a broken world *for* heaven, but to be people who are transforming the present world to be more *like* it.

If people believe the world is ending, they'll spend their time preparing for the end of the world; but if people believe they are on an unstoppable mission to change and beautify the world, they'll spend their time doing exactly that. These two choices of how to view the future will have a serious effect on our present behavior, even if we don't consciously intend them to. We can prepare for a horrible ending, or we can prepare for a beautiful beginning, but we can't do both. Those of us who have begun to move out of the Americanized version of Christianity must choose between retaining a pessimistic, fear-based view of the future or learning to dream again. Judging by the difference between how these two competing choices drive behavior historically— Christian disengagement versus working to bring God's peace and reconciliation to everyone—the choice is a critical one. Just as anxiety in one area of life has the power to become a generalized anxiety that spreads throughout all of life, so too does fear about the future direction of the story have the power to lull us into doubt, detachment, and negativity in the here and now.

During my spiritual crisis, sifting back through what I no longer believed about future events proved to be a powerful and logical step in navigating my way beyond a fear-based faith. If I no longer believed in an angry God who is going to burn alive the vast majority of humans who have ever lived, and if I believed that God's story is actually a beautiful, love-filled narrative, then I no longer believed in a horrible ending to God's story. If I no longer believed in a horrible ending to God's story, then I no longer believed there would be some unavoidably negative direction to *my own story*.

It Has Never Been About Escaping

This moment perhaps more than any other became a turning point in my journey. When I let go of those horrific end times, I came to better appreciate how those of us with fundamentalist backgrounds have lots of baggage—baggage that we at times don't even know we're carrying. The subconscious desire to escape to someplace better instead of really embracing the present moment for what it has to offer is one of those pieces of baggage that sticks with us even after we relinquish what we no longer believe about the end times. We can reject bad theology without recognizing and rejecting the bad *implications* of that theology; that takes time and self-awareness to sort out, but it is a critical step that we must do. And when we do it, we stumble upon an invitation that is far better than the invitation to escape: we are given the invitation to steer our stories, and even the story of the whole world, to a more beautiful ending than we previously dared to dream.

A while back I took my then thirteen-year-old daughter Johanna to see the Disney movie *Tomorrowland*. In this movie I unexpectedly stumbled upon a perfect illustration of the unintended consequences of embracing fear-based eschatology versus a hope-filled view of the future. The movie's leading character is Casey Newton, and whenever Casey touches a lapel pin with the letter *T* on it, she instantly finds herself transported to a world called Tomorrowland. For dreamers like Casey, Tomorrowland is an alternate plane of reality where dreamers and thinkers have gathered together to build and create whatever they can imagine—it is a land full of beauty and new creation.

But as Casey soon discovers, with the help of Frank Walker, the technological advances in Tomorrowland have somewhat backfired, as the Tomorrowland dreamers had built a future-telling machine. This future-telling machine was foretelling the unavoidable and soon-to-unfold end of the world. The machine was also broadcasting that signal to those outside of Tomorrowland, causing their unconscious minds to soak in the message that the world is heading in a progressively worse direction, leading them to believe that nothing can be done to stop it. To this point in time, all of the dreamers and thinkers of Tomorrowland had found themselves unable to figure out how to avoid the end of the world—the clock was ticking in their minds, and nothing was going to be able to stop a destructive future from unfolding. The machine was broadcasting fear, and fear has a way of freezing people until they stand still and passively allow the messages of fear to come true.

The climactic moment of the movie is when Casey flat-out

rejects the prediction of the world's end and simply refuses to believe it—becoming the first official dreamer to discard the doom-and-gloom narrative being spit out by the future-telling machine. Casey eventually confronts the leadership of Tomorrowland and essentially asks, "What if this machine isn't foretelling the future but is instead broadcasting it? What if the world is only ending because everyone is starting to believe the machine's message?" The leader of Tomorrowland, who turns out to be the story's villain, finally admits that Casey is exactly correct—the world is ending *only because everyone believes it is ending* and because they start to act in accordance with that narrative. In a profoundly truthful admission he explains the reason to Casey: "Do you want to know why they believe this message? Because it requires nothing of them *today*."

Let's think about that for a minute: a pessimistic, fear-based view of the future *requires nothing of us today*. If God's story is on a negative course that cannot be altered, and if we believe that our stories are somehow going to end badly no matter what choices we make, then nothing is required of us beyond sitting back and letting it all fall apart. Believing that the world is getting progressively worse and that nothing can be done to change it absolves us of all culpability when we sit back and let it happen. At least, we *think* it absolves us—but I say, it implicates us in the fact that we did *nothing* about it when we had the chance.

As I processed this climactic moment of the movie, I came to see that both my eschatology and my pessimism about where my new spiritual journey was going to lead me was the easiest road I could travel—because letting life and faith fall apart requires no effort. One can just sit back and let it happen and then wallow in the self-pity of believing that nothing could have been done to prevent it.

Back to the movie for a minute. Since I've already spoiled so much of the plot, I'll just go ahead and tell you how it ends: Casey and her friends realize that the only way to save the future of the world is to deconstruct the machine that is persuading everyone that things are getting worse. And they do it. By stopping the broadcasting of the message that the world is ending, they stop the world from ending—because the whole thing was a self-fulfilling prophecy born of a hopeless narrative. When people believed that the world was spiraling out of control, they behaved in accordance with that narrative. When the machine stopped telling them how bad things were, people were free to dream again and build a better future. In fact, in the final moments of the movie, we see a new crop of Tomorrowland recruiters go forth with the express task of "finding the ones who haven't quit dreaming" and who just might hold the ideas and dreams that would make the world a more beautiful place.

This movie, perhaps unintentionally, told the story of the evangelical relationship with a fear-based view of the future. The early evangelicals in the United States were like the original dreamers of Tomorrowland—optimistic, hopeful, and working to build something beautiful, as they prepared for the day Jesus would return to this earth to rule his kingdom of peace. Yet, when they weren't looking, John Nelson Darby came along, and like the machine in Tomorrowland, he started broadcasting the message that the world was getting worse and worse and that the only Christian hope was to one day escape before things got *really* bad. As Darby's message caught on, and as others started broadcasting it and getting rich off it, American Christianity slowly came to a place where it actually started to believe the negative message. Therefore, Christian engagement today isn't quite what it was among the early nineteenth-century evangelicals. Today, we find many Christians openly advocating for one destructive war after another; the environment we rely on for life is slowly being poisoned to death; and the message of Darby—at least the "things will get worse and worse" part of it—seems to be coming true on many levels. I believe this is deeply rooted in the reality that we let a machine (a theological narrative) persuade us that we have no hope other than escaping the downward spiraling story for someplace else.

When we become tempted to believe the worst about God's story, we have a tremendous ability to subtly begin thinking the worst about our own story as well, and I became increasingly aware that I needed to let go of this. When we buy into helpless pessimism and the promise of escape in the grand narrative, we feel silently invited to buy into hopelessness in our own narrative—and that hopelessness leads us to attempt to escape our lives in our own unique ways instead of embracing and transforming our lives. And this was the trap I fell into: because I believed the very worst about God's story, I actually began to believe the worst about my own story as well. As I lay in bed one morning, depressed and feeling like I was suffocating, I realized that I could no longer believe in either of those stories—because if I kept believing them, *I'd keep acting in ways that would invite it all to come true.* Instead, I'd choose to become a person who dared to dream again—even if I was wrong in daring to dream such things about life.

Where Have All the Dreamers Gone?

The movie *Tomorrowland* ends with a quest to discover and recruit all the dreamers who haven't quit dreaming yet, and I couldn't help but wonder about the same thing for American Christianity: Where have all the dreamers gone? It seems that Christianity in the United States was at one time ripe with dreamers—people who believed that the trajectory of God's story was moving in a beautiful direction and that all of our individual stories were beautiful mini-narratives that fit within the grander narrative arc. Throughout history, time and time again, we have seen that the presence of dreamers who dare to keep dreaming ends up changing the world and making it a little more like heaven in the here and now.

But more than American Christianity in general, what I really wanted to know was where the dreamer had gone who used to be inside *me*. For some chapters of my life I was full of dreams and full of hope—I certainly started out as one of the dreamers. Yet, through the hustle and bustle and monotony of everyday life, through the pain of adopting four children but only getting to raise one of them, through marital struggles and failures, through losing a church and an entire circle of friends during a dark life chapter, and amid a crisis of faith that left me rethinking everything, that dreamer inside of me died. He caved in to the fear that it wasn't going to be okay in the end.

The most toxic and damaging theology we can hold is the theology that kills our dreams and replaces optimism and hope with pessimism and fear. While I had technically let go of this pessimistic view of the future long before some of my more recent, darker moments, I realized that simply naming what I no longer believed, in this case, wasn't enough. When it came to the issue of pessimism and fear of the future, I had to go one step farther and name the part of me that this type of theology killed: the dreamer.

I don't know where all the dreamers have gone, but I do know that wherever they are, I want to be counted among them. As

Paul the apostle once said, I want to know the power of the resurrection—I want to know the power of feeling the dreamer inside of me brought back and given new life. Of all the things that drained the life out of me during my crisis of faith, the fact that I had slowly lost the desire or the energy to dream was perhaps the worst—and not dreaming is something I simply cannot return to, no matter the cost. For me, reclaiming the freedom to dream again was born from the realization that the invitation of Jesus was never an invitation to escape the world, but to transform it into something beautiful—and that requires *dreaming*. It was never about going somewhere else, but about bringing a little more of that somewhere else into the everyday world around us.

This is what makes holding a pessimistic view of God's story or our own so heretical: it divides us and separates us from the mission we've been assigned in this world. In fact, if someone wanted to derail a movement of God's people from their dedication to making the world a little more like heaven every day, the best way to do it would be to persuade them that the story is all going to end badly regardless of their efforts.

The world doesn't need any more fear-based pessimists. We don't need any more blood moon books, we don't need even one more rapture teacher, we don't need any more "Christian" movies predicting that the world is about to end in a hail of gunfire, and we certainly don't need any more versions of that crazy uncle you probably have who claims to have the prophecy of the seventy weeks of Daniel understood to an exact science. What we do need is a new generation of dreamers—people who see the vast expanse between the kingdom of heaven and the day-to-day world we live in and who know that there's a lot of dreaming and conspiring to be done if we're to make this place look a little more like heaven before we die.

The world doesn't need any more skeptics, knee-jerk critics, pessimists, or general downers. It needs dreamers, thinkers, and coconspirators who are dedicated to bringing a bit more of heaven to earth in the here and now—and who don't let fear get in the way.

My prayer is that we in the American church will turn away from the recently built machine that is broadcasting our imminent departure and the world's pending demise. We must not pray "thy kingdom come, thy will be done on earth as it is in heaven" unless we're actually willing to live in accordance with the reality that it *has come* and that *it is done*. The task of building God's kingdom, on earth as it is in heaven, as we await the return of our eternal king is a beautiful task that can be fully embraced only by those who haven't quit dreaming yet. As in Tomorrowland, once the doom-and-gloom machine is dismantled, we just might find ourselves free to go out and conspire to do good with other dreamers who are dedicated to making this present world a better place for everyone and everything.

Because once we no longer believe in a pessimistic view of God's story or our own? Well, once we no longer believe that, we're invited to begin dreaming again and to find a million possibilities to replace what we have let go of. It was this realization, staring my negativity machine in the face, that caused me to fully understand that perhaps, just perhaps, my spiritual midlife crisis wasn't so much about the death of dreams, but the birth of them.

You and I were created for more than pessimism and suiting up for our departure. We were made to dream big things, and then to go do them.

6.

FOLLOWING JESUS INSTEAD OF THE TRIBE

One of the things I've learned is that turning from fear and awakening to love naturally gives way to an optimistic view of life and the future, and adopting optimism invites us to begin rethinking everything about life and the world around us. Here were some of the epiphanies I had: if God is not an ISIS terrorist but the extreme version of the person who loves us most; if the Bible is a document designed to point us toward the embodiment of God's love as found in the person of Jesus; if we were created by love to reflect and receive love; and if God's story is one that's moving in a beautiful direction where I get to be a player—then I was all in. I was ready to get busy spreading some love and beauty around the world.

However, here's the problem I quickly ran into: participation in the Christian mission around the world isn't a solo activity—it's a team sport. I realized I needed to rethink how I viewed other Christians. What began as a mission between a team of twelve assembled by Jesus has now spread around the world and back again—and we're actually supposed to be working in unity with one another. In fact, this is the last thing Jesus prayed for before he was arrested—that all those who believed in him would be unified. Sadly, in Americanized Christianity "unified" is pretty much the last word I can think of anyone using to describe us.

I had a growing realization of and appreciation for this disunity in the church as I became more and more aware of all the things I no longer believed. It seemed as if each time I shed a belief and started over with what was left in the wake, I had a keen sense that I just didn't know where I fit in anymore. My new faith experience was leading me to some beliefs, and some disbeliefs, that I knew would put me at odds with everyone to some degree or another. Some people accused me of being conservative; others accused me of being a slave to the left. To plenty of others (here's looking at you, random people who post on the Internet), I wasn't even a #TrueChristian anymore. It was as if everyone seemed to know what I was and where I fit—except me.

To be honest, although hope and optimism had set in, this was the most lonely part of the journey as I searched and searched for a perfect place to call my spiritual home—one that I had never found among the options of American Christianity. In fact, as I tried out different groups, thinking that perhaps I had arrived at my destination, there were always plenty of voices reminding me that I didn't fit within the tribe, for whatever reason. Sometimes one of those voices was even mine, as I secretly had misgivings about groups that did accept me (such as when I realized that progressive flavors of Christianity can gravitate toward fundamentalism every bit as much as conservative flavors of Christianity).

I felt like I was outside in the church parking lot, unsure which direction to head. Yet, as discouraging as this felt, standing outside in the church parking lot was a familiar place for me, as in addition to being the former King of Bible Memorization, I actually have a rich history of getting myself chased out of churches in one way or another, thanks to guns, gays . . . and *tattoos*.

Chased Out into the Church Parking Lot

I was all of seventeen years old the first time I was chased out of church. When I say "chased out," I'm not using some exaggerated metaphor for being asked politely to leave; instead, I was actually *chased out into the parking lot*. It was one of those Thursday evenings where, let's just say, church youth group didn't go exactly as anyone had planned. That night, there wouldn't be any eating doughnuts off a string with our hands tied behind our backs (enhanced by the ambiance of Michael W. Smith's "Friends" playing in the background). Whatever was planned for that night was about to be massively derailed by my ill-timed revelation that I was now intimately familiar with a man who was simply known as the Mad Hatter.

I have no idea what his real name is or was; we teenagers in town just knew him as the Mad Hatter. He was an elderly man who owned a tattoo shop in Old Orchard Beach, Maine, called—you guessed it—the Mad Hatter Tattoo Shop. Though I never saw him without his shirt on, word on the street was he got the nickname because he had an entire backpiece of the Mad Hatter from *Alice in Wonderland*. He had a reputation for being an old-school tattooer who they said was among the best of the best from his generation—a claim I believed until he tattooed me. More important for me at the time was another reputation he had: he was where you went if you were underage and wanted to get a tattoo with little hassle. I guess you could say I was a well-rounded teenager; I was the kid who could beat the Sunday School teachers at a sword drill, but I was also the kid who knew where to go when you needed to get inked and didn't have a fake ID. I was resourceful like that.

I was scared out of my mind on the day I finally walked into the Mad Hatter's parlor to attempt to get my first tattoo. I thought my heart was going to jump out of my chest as I pointed to an image on the wall of a heart with a cross going through it and said, "I'd like to get that, please." I was trying to act all calm and cool, as if I were just some adult biker who had walked in confidently to touch up some prison ink.

What can I say? I was cool and lame all at the same time back then.

The Mad Hatter quoted me the price of twenty-five bucks, but my heart sank when he said, "But I'll need to see some ID." *That* was a problem. I told him I'd need to run back to my car to grab it, so I walked back to my car debating whether I'd return and try to pull this off or just drive away and chalk up my first tattoo attempt as a loss. "This isn't like trying to buy cigarettes," I thought to myself, as there weren't a dozen other tattoo shops I could just keep trying until someone took the cash without asking for ID. This was my one shot.

Pushing through my anxiety (I was fearless, remember?), I returned with my laminated high school identification (you know, the ones that literally had a cutout photo laminated on top of a piece of construction paper), which had just my name on it—no date of birth. I confidently handed it to him and said, "This is all I have for ID, but I'm eighteen, I swear." As he handed my school ID card back to me, he sat down in his chair without saying a word and began putting a needle into his tattoo gun (and I've since learned that you're not actually supposed to call it a tattoo gun, but I do anyway). I knew I was golden and walked out of that shop with what remains my lamest tattoo ever: a heart and a cross on my right hip (so that my mom wouldn't find out, because she had threatened that if I got a tattoo before I was eighteen she'd scrub it off with a Brillo pad).

Well, I *thought* I was golden until I decided to show everyone at youth group what was now my prized possession. That, let's just say, didn't go over so well in the end.

I was sort of surprised how it all went down, really. I had expected the adults to tell me how getting a tattoo when you're a teenager is a bad idea, or perhaps to give me a more forceful talking to, but they responded quite kindly. (I still think fondly of the youth leaders after all these years. If any of you are reading this, sorry that I turned out to be such a liberal.) The other kids were split on the thing. Some thought that I was pretty badass for doing it, while others expressed the opinion that it probably wasn't one of the best decisions I'd made that week. All in all, it was a positive reaction: to those who secretly dreamed of breaking free from their parents' oversight, I had become a legend in my own time. To most of the others, I was just that kid in youth group who was always full of surprises.

The reaction was relatively subdued and even somewhat positive, with one exception: my friend Mike. To put it mildly, Mike was pissed sideways about the whole thing.

He was just seventeen years old as well, but it quickly became apparent that he had a lifetime of pent-up fury inside that short little body—fury that he unloaded on me when he found out that I had myself a little tattooage going on.

Within minutes, the "conversation" Mike initiated with me in the foyer of the church spiraled into a death cycle of him shaking a Bible and repeatedly reciting Leviticus 19:28 ("You shall not make any gashes in your flesh for the dead or tattoo any marks upon you: I am the Lord"), followed by me repeatedly saying, "But that's the Old Testament, Mike." Before long, he was growing increasingly animated and shouting at me, so at the prompting of one of the leaders, I headed out to my car to go home. Mike had clearly had a couple of fuses blow inside and wasn't content to let me walk away quietly, so he chased me out, yelling and screaming, "YOU SHALL NOT TATTOO YOUR BODY. I AM THE LORD! I AM THE LORD!" He didn't even catch his breath long enough for me to point out the irony that he was wearing clothing of mixed fibers—but I digress.[1]

At that moment I had little idea that what had transpired that evening would be such a prophetic metaphor of how the future of my Christian experience would go down, but unfortunately, being chased into the church parking lot is almost a guaranteed eventual outcome for those who truly begin to explore what lies beyond the horizon of a fear-based faith. Regardless of how you would describe or label your faith, the reality is that just about all of us live out our faith in the context of social groups—a denomination, a particular church, or a general "circle of people" we run with. Regardless of what kind of group we run with, fear is the glue that keeps the group together. Fear keeps everyone in somewhat conformity with group norms, because fear of being excluded, forced out, or ostracized acts as chains on our hearts and minds to prevent us from thinking or doing anything the group does not approve of.

To truly embrace a life that is beyond fear-based faith, we have to better understand how fear within the context of our faith or social circles controls us, and how fear closes the door to a wide-open life that can appreciate the rich diversity of all that God is doing in the world.

Beyond Christian Tribalism

Christianity in the United States today strikes me as being incredibly tribal, that is, it involves the grouping of similar people to protect against perceived threats from outside or from those belonging to other tribes. Christian tribalism thrives on making new members conform to whatever degree is possible and expelling them if it starts to become apparent that they can't be safely trusted to operate within the boundaries the tribe has set to determine who is a good conservative, a good progressive, or a good whatever. *All tribes do this,* which is why during my faith shift I grew to disdain Christian tribalism and strict adherence to labeling entirely. It doesn't matter if a Christian tribe has a conservative or liberal name; *the destructive aspects of tribalism are all the same.* Those who cannot be trusted to faithfully conform to all of the tribal norms need to be quickly dispatched—anything less is a threat to the homogeneity of the tribe.

When we begin exploring the beautiful possibilities that exist in a love-centered faith, those people who still operate from a place of fear will quickly catch on. We often quietly and unsuspectingly find ourselves pushed to the margins until we wake up and realize—as did I that Thursday evening in the church parking lot—that we're standing in the parking lot when moments before we were safely inside, protected by the walls of the tribe and its members. Other times, we're firmly taken by the arm, marched out to our cars, and told to get lost in a more overt expulsion from the group. Similar scenarios can play out in a host of other ways. Tribal politics and behaviors generate many different ways to push someone out—because fear demands we eliminate that which triggers our fear. Regardless of the "how" or "why," a steady flow of people out into the parking lot is a *natural byproduct of tribalism* regardless of what *kind* of tribalism we're talking about. It's how tribes work, and why Christian tribalism in particular is so toxic to living out the Christian faith.

I can't think of anything that has divided the people of Jesus more than the way we in American Christianity divide ourselves along these strict tribal lines that leave a growing number of us wandering around in the church parking lot. It's as if we are taught from an early age that it's not enough for us to simply say we are Christians; we have to go a step farther and initiate a list of questions to figure out what *kind* of Christian we are—usually with the unspoken premise that we, and others, are trying to find out whether we are a True Christian. If someone gets even one of the answers wrong, that person can easily be seen as a threat because new ideas always have a way of triggering fear in those who aren't ready to be open to them.

I became more aware of this need to hyperidentify and draw my own arbitrary lines during a strange encounter with a fellow Christian at one point during my rediscovery of myself. Upon meeting me, the gentleman wondered whether he could ask me a few questions so that he could figure out what kind of Christian I was. For some reason I agreed—and ended up quickly regretting my decision because the two questions out of his mouth were, "Do you spank your kids?" and "Do you think gays go to hell?"

As soon as he asked the questions I was, like, "Wait—what the hell kind of survey is this?" I should have known this True Christian Survey wasn't going anywhere, but in that moment I was foolish enough to answer his questions. When I answered no on both counts, and answered another question to indicate I also no longer believed in the rapture, the gentleman told me that the reason why I was an adoptive father instead of a biological father was because God was refusing to bless me with children.

I suppose statistically speaking there are some people in this world who have never been punched square in the face. More specifically, I can tell you that the only reason some of these folks have never been punched square in the face is because I believe in nonviolence. This is also true for the gentleman who thought that being the father of two wonderful children from Peru was somehow less than a blessing from God, as my dedication to nonviolence spared him that day, but just barely. While this interaction was an extreme example of the way we try to figure out "what kind" of Christian someone is, the rest of us have a way of doing it, too—even if in less punch-worthy ways.

As I became aware of our propensity for doing this, I realized more and more that I no longer believed in the importance of belonging to any particular Christian group, or even identifying with any particular description of what kind of Christian I was. I no longer wanted to be held in the grip of fear that subtly controlled what I was willing to think, explore, or believe because I was afraid of upsetting the group and being pushed out of it. For me, all of those things were forces that drained life from my faith instead of enhancing the vitality of it. Furthermore, once I got a taste of faith beyond my standard horizons, I realized there really wasn't a word or a particular tribe that completely described me anymore.

Those of us who feel stuck in the parking lot among all the various Christian tribes arrived there by way of our own individual stories and unique circumstances. Some of these experiences were traumatic and painful expulsions from groups, and some were simply situations where we experienced a gradual paradigm shift over time that led us to the place where we just didn't quite fit anywhere anymore. Regardless of how we made it out into the parking lot, however, we all face the same question once we get to our cars, and this question is perhaps one of the most important questions we will ever face: *What do we do now?*

This is an important question, and one that I pondered many mornings lying in my bed far later than I probably should have. I had spent so much of my spiritual journey bouncing between church parking lots and trying on new labels to define myself that I had made myself miserable—never having given myself the space to be fully me, or fully who God wanted me to be. Many times I was like those friends we all have who can't stand to not be in a relationship, so they jump into a new one the minute they leave the old one—only to repeat their history over and over again. I wasn't sure where to go next, but I knew I didn't want to live that way anymore—I just wanted to be *me* for the first time in my life.

If you're a "parking-lot Christian" who has found yourself no longer fitting in neatly with a Christian tribe or label, I think the best thing you can do for the moment is—well, *nothing.* That sounds like horrible advice, but let me explain: sometimes doing nothing gives us enough space to breathe so that we can learn to make better decisions and think rationally again. Feeling like we don't fit can be an extremely uncomfortable position, and our instinct is often to relieve that tension by forcing ourselves to fit somewhere else, even when we don't (and we often feel compelled to do this quickly, which only exacerbates the situation). For me, doing nothing—realizing that I didn't have to be any particular type of Christian right now and that I didn't have to be afraid of that—gave me the freedom to rediscover myself and to find a better expression of faith, without someone else doing the defining for me.

Many times, we leave one tribe and their behaviors for a new tribe, thinking we've somehow been enlightened or embraced progress, but then we simply adopt the *same tribal behaviors under a new banner*. This option invites us into the same old cycle, which we already know doesn't work and already know leaves us dissatisfied. Other times, we walk completely away from a functional faith as we throw up our hands in disgust over what we've experienced in whatever tribal expression of Christianity we grew dissatisfied with.

I've lived this pattern, so I know it well. When I was a fundamentalist, I became like the fundamentalists. When I was a progressive, I became like the progressives. I became a lot of things as I navigated my crisis of faith—except for *me*. In the end, I realized that *me* was the only thing I was interested in being—because it was the only way I was going to find peace. My life got instantly better the moment I accepted that I didn't have to fit perfectly anywhere on the Christian landscape, and that this would be okay.

From my experience on both extremes, I've learned enough to say with confidence that the key to moving forward and finding a better expression of Christian faith must start with rejecting the lie that landing neatly within any one particular Christian camp is where we need to land. In fact, I went on to realize that trying to fit within a Christian label was one of the very things that made me feel crazy so much of the time—because that's what labels do to Christians. They invite us to live in a subtle fear, and that makes us act crazy. Like, *really, really crazy*.

The Crazy-Making Power of a Christian Label

Between the era of the Protestant Reformation and the current reformation that is transitioning the church past Christendom lies an era I like to call the Era of Christian Tribalism. The once "Church Universal" is now fractured into thousands of groups and in need of voices of reason to help us collectively move beyond our broken and divisive history.

We Christians today are in a valuable position to help Christianity move beyond this era of tribalism as we rethink the way we've drawn lines that even Jesus himself did not draw and as we continuously expand the boundaries to invite more and more people in. Our past obsessions with in versus out, right versus left, and us versus them have created a cultural Christian environment that is often nearly as toxic as the typical climate on Capitol Hill. Life beyond a fear-based faith, then, becomes an invitation for us to partner with Jesus in becoming the kinds of Christians who express a Christianity that is beyond all of the words and labels that exist in our particular culture.

At the heart of Christian tribalism, one will always find a label. These labels will be neatly defined at the forefront of Christian identity and will often be used to separate and divide the institution usually thought of as the "body" of Christ. Sadly, our obsession with labels has existed since the inception of the church, as seen in the New Testament. In fact, some people in the early church were dividing themselves based upon who was following Paul and who was following Apollos, which the Apostle Paul rightly rebukes (1 Cor 3:4),[2] pointing them back to the truth that this deal was all about following Jesus, *not a label*.

The labels used to define "Christian" that started in the early church continued to divide Christians for the rest of church history, at some points more than others. Ecumenical councils sorted through some of these issues, and creeds were developed to define the only label that ever really mattered—that of "Christian." But since we are addicts of labels, these creeds were not enough, so we developed even *more* labels to divide people into groups on the basis of how they *understood* the creeds and to determine who was, or was not, a heretic (that is, someone who taught something that disagreed with the creeds). Then, in 1517, we see the final ignition that lit the Reformation when Luther nailed his ninety-five theses to that famous church door, and a new reformation was ushered onto the Christian scene.

For whatever value came of the Reformation, it certainly sparked some changes on the Christian landscape that were not all net-positive results. Before the Reformation, although the church had some horrific behaviors and there was plenty of fighting over who was in and who was out, at least there was more of a sense of the "Church Universal" or the global church. This appreciation of the Church Universal—the understanding that all of Christ's followers are ultimately part of the same body, even when they hold opposing viewpoints on various matters—seemed to get lost. Heck, we even started burning alive in town squares the Christians we didn't agree with, so I guess you could say that an appreciation for theological diversity was, well, *absent.*

In the centuries since the Reformation, the Church Universal has become more than an estimated forty thousand separate Christian tribes, many of which no longer see the others as being part of the Church Universal at all. (In fairness, 39,564 of them are probably just some form of a Baptist church, born out of a church business meeting gone wrong.) Certainly, diversity of Christian thought and expression is a good thing, and much good has come from many of the denominations or tribes that have been born since the Reformation. However—and here's the kicker—with diversity comes the need to have an individualized Christian label by which to define our group, and with that new way of defining ourselves or our group—*combined* with a loss of appreciation for the Church Universal—comes the poison of Christian tribalism.

Back in the day, if you wore the wrong Christian label you might get punched in the face for being a heretic, as happened when St. Nicholas got mad at the First Ecumenical Council in 325 CE. By the year 380 official laws were enacted stating that any Christian identifying with the wrong Christian label was to have his or her property confiscated and, if possible, to be destroyed (killed). Fast-forward to 1076, when Ramihrdus of Cambrai became the first person burned for allegedly being a heretic, thereby ushering in a good long era of burning fellow Christians alive. Just a few years later, we see the beginning of the lovely tradition of hanging heretics and *then* burning them, as if one execution method were not enough. By the seventeenth century we learned to embrace our inner creativity, along with appreciating the days of old, and returned to crucifying heretics upside down, stuffing their mouths with gunpowder that was then ignited, or slowly bleeding people to death. What can I say? When it came to killing fellow Christians who used the wrong label or believed the wrong things, we were pretty dedicated to doing the deed—and doing it as creatively as possible.

Today, things aren't quite as extreme, but we do still figuratively burn people at the stake who wear the wrong labels—by using hateful words on the Internet or withholding relationships (getting shunned from a particular Christian circle). I mean, let's be honest: modern stake burning is how the word "farewell" became almost an iconic cultural statement on the Christian Internet.

Speaking of "farewelling," I was again reminded of this after watching what felt like a public trial for capital punishment when evangelical author and speaker Jen Hatmaker revealed that she believed in welcoming LGBTQ individuals fully into the church.

Many months after facing the wrath of the "Christian Machine," as Jen called it, she described what it was like to be considered a modern heretic who was figuratively burned at the stake in those modern ways:

> This year, I deeply experienced being on the wrong side of religion, and it was soul-crushing. I suffered the rejection, the fury, the distancing, the punishment, and sometimes worst of all, the silence. I experienced betrayal from people I thought loved us. I felt the cold winds of disapproval and the devastating sting of gossip. I received mocking group texts about me, accidentally sent to me; "Oh, we were just laughing WITH you!" they said upon discovery, an empty, fake, cowardly response. It was a tsunami of terror. One hundred things died. Some of them are still dead. Some are struggling for life but I don't know if they will make it. . . .
>
> This year I became painfully aware of the machine, the Christian Machine. I saw with clear eyes the systems and alliances and coded language and brand protection that poison the simple, beautiful body of Christ. I saw how it all works, not as an insider where I've enjoyed protection and favor for two decades, but from the outside where I was no longer welcome. The burn of mob mentality scorched my heart into ashes, and it is still struggling to function, no matter how darling and funny I ever appear; the Internet makes that charade easy.[3]

What happened to Jen Hatmaker was painful to witness, but tragically, it happens every day in Christianity. It happens in fundamentalism, and it happens in progressive Christianity. Tribalism is ugly, and it's everywhere.

The bottom line is that *Christian labels have a way of making us crazy,* which is precisely why we need to reform our understanding of the tribal labels that drive us to inflict wounds instead of working to heal them. To embrace a faith that is freeing and life-giving, we need to understand this potential crazy-making power of Christian labels so that we can lead the Church Universal, and ourselves, into a new era that moves beyond this obvious fear of "the other." Now, to be clear, the issue is rarely the labels themselves but *how we relate to the labels* that start to form us into people who look like *anything but* the Jesus of the New Testament.

Rethinking How We Use Christian Labels

As I continued to rethink who I was as a person, and wrestled with all those things I no longer believed, I asked myself the question, "But what *kind* of Christian am I?" I tried to answer this question for my own self and realized that Christian labels aren't entirely bad; in some ways they can actually be useful. We live in a culture that compartmentalizes many things, so labels help us navigate the world around us by helping us understand how things fit and relate to one another. For example, the labels "Roman Catholic" and "Protestant" help us to identify whether an individual holds to the pre-Reformation Christian tradition or is part of a tradition that is a product of the Reformation. Using a label like this to gain a basic navigational orientation (absent judgments of good or bad) is not harmful but potentially useful. As with most things in life, it is not the thing itself that is the problem but the ways in which we use it that gets us into trouble. In my personal journey, this didn't come to mean that I needed to abandon all labels whatsoever but that I became conscious of the ways labels can be dangerous, misused, and ultimately harmful, both to myself and to those around me.

In this regard it is important to understand that Christian labels can be useful tools but can also be incredibly dangerous. Sometimes we must handle labels with the most delicate gloves. Just like a power tool can help make life better and easier if used properly and under necessary guidance, but can become harmful and destructive when not, Christian labels should have a tag affixed that warns, "Use with extreme caution and under close supervision."

Christian labels ought to be one of those things that we encourage people to understand and know how to use properly before they run off on their own and start wielding them freely. We recognize this need with many other tools that can be useful when used properly but dangerous and harmful when accidentally misused or purposely abused. For example, cars are very useful tools if used safely in a way that does not put anyone in danger; but they can be used dangerously, too. For some reason, we forget to see both useful and harmful sides of *words*. In my experience of having both misused labels and had them misused against me, I've discovered a few key principles for you to consider as you move forward on your spiritual journey.

First, we must be aware of the powerful force a label has to *shape identity*. People who improperly use them (sometimes not intentionally but through a lack of self-awareness) tend to begin drawing and enjoying a sense of identity, meaning, and purpose not from Christ, but from the label and the group that label represents. Subtly, over time, our lives become shaped and driven by our identity as "evangelical," "Calvinist," "progressive," or other labels. The label, which doesn't represent Christ but represents an imperfect filter through which we view Christ, becomes the core of our understanding of self *without our even realizing it.* We have a tendency to get so caught up in who the label tells us we are, and what the label tells us we should think and do, that the label itself *functionally becomes God.* That's straight idolatry no matter which way you slice it.

As followers of Jesus of Nazareth we are invited to get our identity and sense of meaning from him, and him alone. We are invited to drop our nets and follow him, to take on his yoke and to understand who we are, through him. Our core identity, like that of the earliest disciples, must be completely consumed with simply being one of his followers—people created by love, in the image of love, for the purpose of receiving and reflecting love. Drawing identity from any source other than Jesus is a fleeting endeavor. It cannot sustain us in the long term; it will leave us spiritually dehydrated and ultimately lead to a million forms of spiritual death.

We see Jesus warn the crowd of this early in his public ministry when he tells them that although they know the Scriptures inside and out, they have missed the fact that all Scripture points to him. Jesus ends with, "Yet you refuse to come to me to have life" (John 5:40). When Christian labels become the object that gives us identity and understanding of self, we become like the religious leaders of Jesus's time—people who are highly religious in a false sense because it's a religion of the label, not of Jesus. Simply put, getting identity from our Christian label, however unintentional, causes us to completely miss out on our true identity—that of a follower of Jesus who was created to receive and reflect love.

Second, when we allow our identities to be defined by tribal labels, we slowly become people compelled to fight for and defend the label, even if it means causing harm to fellow Christians. We do this because any perceived threat to *the label* becomes (in our minds) a threat to *ourselves,* even though this is usually not the case.

Our tribal behaviors in this area often remind me of a scene from Mel Gibson's classic movie *Braveheart.* In the movie, William Wallace (played by Gibson) marries a Scottish woman in secret. At that time, the oppressive English occupiers had instituted a law whereby Scottish brides were raped on their wedding night by English lords, and Wallace refused to allow this to happen to his bride. The English soldiers soon catch on and try to rape her anyway. During the struggle, Wallace's wife, Murron, fights back against the soldiers—a response they don't take to kindly. After the struggle, the soldiers take her to the town center and tie her to a pole to be publicly executed. Speaking to the townspeople witnessing the event, the executioner warns, "An assault on one of the king's soldiers is the same as an assault on the king himself," and then he lifts his knife to take her life.

This scene reminds me of how we often feel unnecessarily defensive when we gain our identity and meaning from Christian labels instead of from Christ. When the label becomes a core way of understanding ourselves, or when we begin to think that our label is the only one that expresses The Real Truth, we experience any threat to that label as an attack not just on ourselves, but on the gospel. A critique of Calvinism becomes a critique of God. A critique of one aspect of American evangelicalism becomes a perceived threat and personal attack, not just against the label, but against our King. No one likes to feel threatened—it is an emotion that taps into our most primal instincts of fight or flight—so we develop behaviors to avoid circumstances that might cause us to feel like our identity and self-preservation are at risk. This practice of preemptively protecting ourselves and other members of the tribe from perceived threats is something I've come to call "policing the boundaries."

The Need to Police the Boundaries

When I was a member of the U.S. Air Force, I had the opportunity to be stationed all around the world and gain an immense amount of life experience. One of the first things I observed was that all military installations are under the threat of some form of attack at any time. One never knows when or whether an attack will occur, but the first line of defense for those inside the base is to have a secure perimeter that is constantly policed by security forces. Boundaries that define the limitations of the installation are determined, and a fence is erected to secure the boundary. Guard shacks are built at every entrance to the base and assigned personnel around the clock to approve each individual who enters. Security forces ride along the fence in ATVs to make sure no threat crosses the barriers. Other security forces are assigned to police the people who are already inside in case someone is discovered who needs to be expelled. All things considered, protecting those inside the walls of a military installation via constant policing of the boundaries is a major priority.

When we allow Christian labels to become our means of identity, and group closely together with others who also share that label (and who draw their identity from it), we quickly gravitate toward a tribal, military mindset: we focus on policing the tribal boundaries to prevent intruders from entering and to expel them if they do, and to make sure that everyone inside belongs there. Instead of being full participants in the metaphor of the Body of Christ, we become an amputated hand doing our own thing—an amputated hand that, no less, only wants to hang out with other amputated hands. We prevent those who "don't belong" from entering in many ways, and when one is discovered to have accidently slipped past the gate, we take swift and decisive action to make sure the rest of the group knows that person doesn't belong (fundamentalists will escort you out, while progressive Christians will publicly shame you until you go away). This deadly and destructive cycle enters into a "lather, rinse, and repeat" death spiral, all because we gravitate toward using labels as a source of life and identity instead of reserving that for Jesus. All tribes have the ability to behave this way, and if you don't believe me, send out a Tweet that isn't in full harmony with your tribe, and I promise, it won't take long for the Twitter Police of that tribe to find you.

Why? Because once you set hard boundaries and draw identity from them, those boundaries *must* be policed. There's no other option.

Beyond a simple policing of the boundaries, we also find that this need to police becomes a need to judge, as the sinful human condition makes it quite difficult to do the former without the latter. This policing and judging, as with other concerns, is not born from the label itself but from our relationship to the label. This is because our Christian labels often carry a subtle or not-so-subtle smugness within the label's subculture that quietly whispers (or in the case of some tribes, loudly whispers), "We get it, and if you're not one of us, you don't get it." When we combine this smug certainty with identity centered on the label instead of on Christ, desires for self-preservation, and a lack of true, empathetic relationships with Christians of other labels, we quickly find ourselves in a life pattern of sinfully judging others on the basis of the label that is or is not associated with them.

As I did some hard internal work and processing around

my relationships to Christian labels, I had to force myself to
constantly return to the truth that judging another person is
wrong—Christ himself clearly forbids it—because none of us has
enough information about someone else's heart to properly judge
that person. Only God can do that. What is especially dangerous
about this type of tribal judging is that it's not even judging
people by the measuring stick of Christ; rather, judgments
are passed that are based on the measuring stick of our own
Christian label. This is one of the most destructive behaviors
that can be found in Christianity: judging, and doing it wrongly
because we are judging according to the prefabricated standards
of a Christian label and not on the basis of Jesus, the founder of
our faith.

When we mix this all together, we find that Christian labels
can be very dangerous tools if used incorrectly. Improperly
drawing our sense of self from them (even unintentionally)
creates idolatrous identity issues, ushers us into a life of policing
boundaries (and thereby withholding relationships), and leads us
to sinfully judge others by the worst possible measuring stick: the
label that created this cycle in the first place. As soon as we start
to gain life and identity from a Christian label, we cross over from
using a tool that is beneficial for cultural compartmentalization to
entering into waters that will ultimately destroy us—*after* they first
destroy other people around us.

Getting identity from a Christian label is a game we simply
can't win. The entire structure of the game is tilted in the house's
favor, and even though we might have some nice stretches, we'll
eventually lose. We were never designed to get our identity, worth,
value, or anything else from a human-made label—because once a
label conveys meaning and becomes synonymous with being right,
we become fearful of anything outside of that label. This is a game

where we are completely doomed the moment we sit down at the table to play.

I don't think Jesus ever intended for it to be this way.

Jesus Really Isn't a Fan of Boats

Refusing to play the label game invites us into a new spiritual journey—one that isn't really new at all and might be better described as a return to the beginning where it all began: emulating Jesus, who was the ultimate expression of love toward others. Drawing identity from any area other than the source of life is a spiritual death sentence, and worse, it's contagious, because it gives birth to tribalism. However, when we return to our central identity of image-bearers designed to receive love from and reflect love to others, we are naturally invited to shed all of the unloving, fear-based tribal behaviors that come from loyalty to the label. Instead of being stuck in in-versus-out debates over a host of secondary issues, we find that shedding labels and returning to our central identity and purpose frees us to begin to love and appreciate the world around us in new and beautiful ways—instead of viewing it with fear and skepticism.

Moving into Christianity beyond the labels frees us in ways that enrich this spiritual journey. The most important is that we have more freedom to follow Jesus into those unlikely places where he loves to show up, instead of being fearfully limited to see him working only within the boundaries where we had expected to find him. When we fall too deeply into an identity that is meshed together with a Christian label, we eventually reach a point where we expect to see Jesus only moving within the lines that we've drawn, because anything else prompts the fear that we might be wrong. Often, we miss Jesus entirely because we're looking for him *here* when really he's out busy doing something *over there*. Moving beyond a label-centered Christian identity allows us to see Jesus do what he does best: the unexpected.

I believe that early on, Jesus wanted to send his followers a strong message to always be open to finding him show up beyond the boundaries that we've laid out for him. While the Gospels describe Jesus as the God-man who performed all kinds of miracles, the most interesting of all those miracles is the only one that doesn't have an obvious reason for or explanation behind it: walking on water in the middle of the night.

For all of the other miracles, one can easily point to a motivator or a reason behind them. Feeding of the five thousand? They were hungry, and Jesus saw that they needed to eat immediately instead of going into town for food. All of the physical healings? Scripture repeatedly says, "And Jesus saw them, and felt compassion for them." But walking on water in the middle of the night? This one is a bit more bizarre, and Scripture doesn't explain what point Jesus was trying to make—we're just left to guess.

As the story goes, the disciples were out on the Sea of Galilee, tossing among the waves during those dark hours of the middle of the night that would give a lot of folks the spooks. As they're bouncing among the waves in their small boat, they see something off in the distance, and once they realize it looks like a person, they freak out and assume they're seeing a ghost.

Except it's Jesus. So the freaking out gives way to some confusion over the situation, because, well, a late-night stroll on the Sea of Galilee isn't exactly where they expect to find Jesus.

Of all the places where they might expect to find Jesus, this was positively the last place on the list. Strike that—this wasn't even *on* the list of potential places where they thought they might find

Jesus. He should have been *anywhere* other than walking on the Sea of Galilee in the middle of the night.

Even after Peter's famous reaction, "Lord, if it is you, command me to come to you on the water" (Matt 14:28), we still don't find out exactly what Jesus's point is. His interaction with Peter about doubting is in reaction to Peter's response, which is *secondary* to whatever the primary point is. Even when the scene is over in the book of Matthew, we still don't see what Jesus is trying to prove or do—we're left guessing. Certainly, he didn't need to prove he had the power to perform miracles; Jesus had already done that more times than the disciples could count. To top it off, the author doesn't even offer an aside saying, "And this was the point of what Jesus said and did," as we see in other parts of Scripture (such as in John 2:21). It's just a crazy story that leaves us guessing about its point.

There's no explanation. Nada.

When I look at the story, I see, at least in part, Jesus trying to appeal to those of us who are visual learners and who need symbolic reminders of deeper truths in order for those truths to stick with us past lunchtime. For me, the story of Jesus walking on water is his way of saying, "Expect the unexpected" (and those *Big Brother* fans out there just heard that part in a Julie Chen voice). It's as if Jesus is giving the disciples a visual lesson to remind them—and us—that he isn't constrained by *our* boundaries and can always be found moving in the most unlikely of places.

Jesus is, and always has been, a person we can expect to be doing things we don't expect him to do, in the places where we don't think he'd be, with the people we didn't think he'd be with. His enemies were those who dedicated themselves to obeying every rule in the Bible. His best friends were sex workers, social misfits, and everyone else the religious leaders had declared were "out." I believe our spiritual journey gets much richer the moment we accept this, and accept that Jesus seems to have not just opted out of our boundary systems entirely, but is actually busy walking behind us and erasing the lines we've drawn. And this is precisely why it is so important to move into a Christian identity that is beyond fear and beyond all the labels: it frees us to find Jesus wherever he is, doing whatever he does, with those he prefers to do it with.

Labels, however unintentionally, have the ability to become our own little tiny boats that limit the way we look for and see God working in the world around us. They're comfortable boats the longer we get used to cruising through life in them as our identity. Over the course of time, everyone in that boat has the human tendency to think that Jesus is inside *that* boat, and *only* that boat. Because we begin to feel so strongly about Jesus existing primarily within the boundaries of our own boat, we become skeptical of all the other boat-riders out there who claim that Jesus is riding in *their* boat, too. Instead of getting everyone from all of the boats together to figure out how we can *all* partner with Jesus to make the world a little less broken and a little more right, we end up sailing around in circles pointing fingers at each other because everyone thinks that Jesus is riding *only* in their own boat. To make it worse, we even point fingers at them because they pointed fingers at us, and somehow we think we're morally superior in the exchange of finger pointing (Exhibit A: the Progressive Christian Twitter Police).

The ultimate reason we do this is because of an unhealthy identity with Christian labels. Labels, when used improperly, convince us of the subtle message that Jesus is more in our boat than he is in someone else's boat. Our goal then becomes how to persuade everyone else to pile into our own boat, instead of looking out on the billows to find where Jesus is and to move in his direction as quickly as possible—even if that means getting *out* of our own boat, or forsaking boats *entirely*.

Whatever truths may be found in the story of Jesus walking on water, I think one of its most important truths is that Jesus isn't necessarily more in our boat than in someone else's—because he doesn't actually need a boat at all. Jesus is, and always has been, beyond the limitations of whatever boundaries we want to contain him within. In fact, if we look at the life and ministry of Jesus as recorded in the Gospel accounts, we see that in nearly everything he does, Jesus is constantly moving beyond established boundaries. You just can't say it enough: Jesus is the one going where people don't expect him to go, doing things people don't expect him to do, and working with people they don't expect him to work with.

Jesus is beyond boats. Beyond labels. Beyond boundaries. It's who Jesus is. It's what Jesus does. Whenever we adopt a label, it means we've automatically excluded the Jesus who is always moving beyond them—and this is exactly why I found myself no longer believing in the importance of identifying with labels. If Jesus is the key to a life-giving faith, and Christian labels separate us from him, then those labels have to go—at least, they did for me.

Just as he did with Peter, Jesus still invites us to be unafraid and to step outside of our comfortable little boats that we've neatly constructed with fine-sounding arguments from dead German philosophers and Greek verbs, and to walk forward into the vast expanse where he is always doing something new—and doing it somewhere beyond the boundaries we previously thought had defined the Son of God's limitations. Those of us who already feel like we don't fit within one of the prefabricated boats are invited to find faith beyond the labels, a faith where we can move beyond an attachment to those labels and just start chasing after Jesus, in whatever strange places we happen to find him.

In my personal journey of attempting to break free of Christian tribalism (one that I'm not always successful at), I realized the destructive force of drawing life and identity from a Christian label both in my own life and in the lives of those around me. Although it is quite difficult to shed labels completely and still function in a world that uses labels as navigational tools, it *is* possible to refuse to play the identity game. Finding peace for myself amid a label-littered Christian landscape meant shedding all labels for a season and starting from scratch, and paying far more attention to the ways a simple word can sucker us into a very destructive way of living. Once we begin drawing life and identity from a Christian label, we slowly find ourselves viewing any threat to the boundaries of the label as a threat to our identity, which quickly leads us into a life of policing the boundaries to protect our comfortable little boat. This nonsense of false identity and becoming perimeter police has a crazy-making power, and before we know it, we find ourselves tying other people to subtly erected stakes as the other people in our little boat—all with the same identity problem—gather around to drop matches at their feet.

By no longer believing in a need to identify with labels and giving myself permission to be the most authentic version of me, I found a new way of living that invites all of us to look out on the horizon in order to see that next strange place where love and beauty are being created and cultivated—and to go chase it. I believe that is precisely the kind of spiritual journey that Jesus is inviting us to embark on—to find a faith that is beyond fear, beyond labels, beyond boundaries, where we can begin to not just discover Jesus, but to embrace ourselves and others.

7.

FAITH DOESN'T COME WITH A BUBBLE SHEET AND A NO. 2 PENCIL

I'm going to tell you something I've never told anyone before in my life. In fact, I've never even said this out loud before—it's something that I've thought only in those quiet moments when I was feeling keenly aware of those things I didn't believe anymore. Here goes: becoming a widely read blogger made me miserable for a season of life. Outwardly, I was successful and growing in influence, but inside, I was ridiculously unhappy, with a spiritual dissatisfaction that grew by the day.

I am convinced that this played no small role in my faith crisis, as expressing my opinions for a living led me to realize how trapped in a deadly divide we are as Americans. Every time I waded into discussion threads on blog posts, the divide became clearer. Both secular culture and Christian culture seem hopelessly oriented in a left-versus-right binary, as if no other options exist. Nearly every issue that comes up is presented to us with two possible positions we can hold on it: one articulated by conservatives and the other articulated by progressives (or liberals, if you prefer). The Conservative Religious Gatekeepers or the Progressive Twitter Police (depending on where you spend your time) will make it clear to you what you're supposed to think on any issues—and they'll make it clear that you are on the outs if you don't pick the option they think you should pick. It's as if we as American Christians have become the most lazy group thinkers in the world, believing that every question has an answer, and that the answers must be picked from one of the prefabricated options handed to us.

Viewing the most important questions in life through the lens of boxed-in answers that are handed to us from our social group is deadly evidence of a fear-based faith, and one that I never want to return to. The reason why this is so connected to fear is because fear naturally restricts our ability to think—and that is fear's precise function. Think about it primitively: You're walking down a dirt path and come across a deadly hissing snake in front of you. In that moment, fear kicks in to try to save your life, and one of the first things it does is restrict your thinking—it blocks out any information that you don't need in that moment. Your mind immediately forgets whatever was on it moments before, and you become restricted in your ability to think creatively and process all of the options that you theoretically have. Instead, fear gives you just a couple of possible answers to choose from. It does this in life-threatening scenarios because in these cases, fear is your friend and is helping you focus on the few options that may get you out of the dangerous situation.

Fear-based faith performs this same function, though the fear is not a friend in this case because it has falsely identified other people and other viewpoints as being deadly threats. Nonetheless, fear-based faith combined with groupthink subconsciously restricts our ability and willingness to consider answers that are beyond the limited, usually binary, options fear presents to us. False binary options tend to go hand in hand with tribalism, and breaking free from the latter will lead you to rejecting the former. When we begin to move into a faith that is beyond fear and beyond labels, and when we no longer believe the importance of getting identity or life from membership in any particular group, we naturally begin to desire more than breaking free from the group—we ultimately will want to break free from *how the group thinks*.

This was perhaps one of my biggest moments during my faith recovery, as I looked back on the various groups and tribes in my life and realized that I not only wanted to resist a label defining me, but I wanted the freedom to begin to think more creatively. Fear-based faith views questions in light of a couple of possible "correct" answers, and for me, a wide-open life and faith means rejecting a system that invites us to wrestle with such important questions in such restrictive ways.

Earlier in my journey I fell into the trap of believing in false binary options and letting tribalism silently coerce me into which option I'd pick. In fact, I had pretty much done that all my life—it's like being stuck in the Matrix and not knowing that the Matrix even exists. As I reworked my faith in a very public way, in my earlier days I found myself feeling as if I had to hold or defend certain views, not because they sat right with my conscience, but because the group would not tolerate anything other than loyalty to the group position. It's as if the group were saying, "You're with us, or you're with them."

I had to struggle greatly with the feelings this triggered inside me, because when I left fundamentalism I thought I had left this type of system. Honestly, when I became a progressive Christian I was shocked to realize that they often had the same black-and-white pattern of thinking, the same level of thought coercion. They were just as likely to become emotional bullies when I disagreed with them as were the fundamentalists from my childhood.

Fear-based thinking *patterns* have a way of following us, even when we arrive at totally new positions. For me, I slowly came to reject the belief that I had to pick between the choices that everyone claimed were the totality of acceptable options. I lived that way for a time, but I didn't want to live that way anymore—I wanted to think differently, and I didn't care if that meant everyone would hate me.

Between being forced to pick one of only two options that at times both suck equally, and feeling the constant pressure not to bring on the wrath of my tribe, I began to feel like I was being restricted from fully being who I was, as well as who God longed for me to become. While labels and tribalism all played a part, the deeper issue I came to wrestle with was this false notion that we have to quietly accept this left-versus-right cultural orientation in American Christianity—an idea that along with so much else, I no longer believed. Instead, I came to believe that when others force us to pick a side and give us only two options, a totally legitimate Christian response is to dismiss the invitation entirely and to become a more independent thinker.

Jesus Would Have Sucked at This Game— Because He Actually Did

In many ways Jesus would have been a horrible politician because political power jockeys—both secular and religious—were the kind of people he didn't play nice with. However, Jesus would have been an awesome politician if one considers the way he answered questions; interviewing him would have been torture for even the most seasoned White House correspondent. If you've ever watched an interview with a politician, regardless of party affiliation, you've probably noticed that they have a tendency to avoid answering questions. Interviewers will ask, reask, reword, and reask the rewording a hundred times yet never get a straightforward answer—a clear yes or no, agree or disagree. Many times, a politician dodging the question can be a sleazy move to get out of telling the truth, but not always. Sometimes, refusing to take a side or give a clear answer is a sign of tremendous wisdom—because it rejects the question that has been packaged to appear as if there are only two possible answers.

When we read the Gospel accounts of Jesus, we learn a lot of things, but we don't fully learn about the religious and political climate in which Jesus found himself living and teaching. Much can be understood from a straight reading of the Gospel accounts, but it is difficult, if not impossible, to fully grasp the depth of his teachings without having a historical understanding of the culture within which he taught. When we crack that door open, even a little, the teachings of Jesus—and even his approach to questions— take on a much greater depth.

As Christians, when we think about first-century Palestine and the time of Christ, we think about Jesus, which is a great starting point. However, Jesus was not the only rabbi around at that time, and he certainly wasn't the most famous of his day. In fact, two other rabbis were incredibly influential in shaping the religious and political climate that became the arena where Jesus's ideas would compete. In the time preceding Jesus's birth, Hillel the Elder was a famous and influential teacher who shaped much of the thought of that time. Like any religious or political leader, Hillel had opponents who countered what he taught—the most notable being a contemporary of Jesus named Shammai. Between the competing views of Hillel and Shammai, Jesus found himself in a culture that had some interesting similarities to ours: there was a divide between left and right, liberal and conservative, and everyone was trying to figure out where Jesus fit on that spectrum. Like today, you were on either one side or the other, and even when you didn't self-identify with a particular camp, others would try to figure out where they should classify you or what label they should slap on you. Some things just don't change.

When we see the religious leaders of Jesus's time try to nail him down on questions, what we're really seeing is them trying to box Jesus in to one of the preexisting binary options of their day. Jesus doesn't fall for it and repeatedly gives them frustrating answers—often presenting his answers as cryptic parables or even asking a new question. Jesus becomes well-known for his demonstration that he does not fit neatly into the usual categories. Time and time again he seems insistent on proving one point: his ways are radically outside any preexisting categories or paradigms.[1]

The whole thing reminds me of taking an exam with a bubble sheet and a No. 2 pencil. Such exams present a question and then offer four possible answers for you to choose from—and those are your only choices. The only correct answer is one of the answers offered to you. These types of exams are incredibly frustrating for me because sometimes the best answer is beyond the prefabricated choices that are handed to us and sometimes I don't want to shade in *any* of the choices I'm offered. Jesus demonstrated this same point: when people handed him a bubble sheet and a No. 2 pencil, he often handed it right back to them—because his answers were beyond the limited options the world was presenting at the time.

"Yes or no—can we stone her, Jesus?"

"Let he who is without sin."

"Yes or no—can we do good work on the Sabbath, Jesus?"

"Sabbath was made for man, not man for the Sabbath."

"Yes or no—tell us, Jesus!"

"Well, it's like an old woman who lost a coin . . .

"Well, let me tell you about ten virgins and their flashlights . . ."

"It's like this guy who hired people for his garden . . . it's like a guy who found a pearl in his box of apples . . ."

Let's put it this way: Jesus was famous for giving really unsatisfying answers.

Jesus lived in a world where people obsessed over answering questions from false binary options, and Jesus repeatedly frustrated them by refusing to let such a system control the way he wrestled with questions.

We live in a Christian landscape that is hyperobsessed with whether people are liberal or conservative to the point where we judge people based upon which box we think they fit into. Meanwhile, both sides tend to carry themselves as if they have a monopoly on piety while simultaneously throwing bombs over the fence at each other. The irony of the current conservative-versus-liberal divide in Christianity is that if most conservatives realized that Jesus taught some pretty liberal stuff, they'd nail him to the cross all over again; and if most liberal Christians realized that Jesus also taught some conservative things, they'd offer to pass the hammer. The truth is, however, that Jesus isn't looking to find another good conservative or another good liberal. He's looking to find kingdom people who are willing to go against the established grain of culture—people willing to end up with strange bedfellows at times and at odds with both sides at other times. He's looking for people to throw away the bubble sheet that limits our options and stunts our thinking. He's looking for people who blaze a trail to carve out a third way—because *that's what he did.*

Instead of weighing in and getting tangled up in every political or culturally religious debate of his day, Jesus simply responded over and over with stories and riddles that went even deeper than the original questions. Each time Jesus did this, he was essentially saying, "Here's why what I am teaching is radically different from the set of predetermined answers you're trying to pick from, and is even beyond the question you're asking." In fact, at the very end of his life as Jesus stood trial under the Roman governor, he dropped the cryptic nature of his answers and declared boldly that his kingdom is "not of this world." It's different. The way of living that Jesus ushered in—kingdom living—is something that cannot be boxed in or co-opted by labels such as "conservative" and "liberal" or any other construct that we could possibly think up. The way of Jesus, by his own testimony, is something that is "otherworldly" and beyond bubble sheets altogether.

Even in his final moments, Jesus resisted being boxed in to someone else's paradigms and gave his final answer to Pilate as "none of the above." His way is simply . . . different. And he's exactly the right model we need for a new kind of Christianity. We need people willing to think, ask, and imagine both questions and answers that are beyond the bubble sheet we're accustomed to.

Relearning What It Means to Be Holy

If there's one thing that moving beyond a fear-based faith taught me, it was that I wanted to be different, or rather, I began to see myself in my full complexity and realized that I *was* different—and I liked it.

I spent a considerable chunk of my life feeling excluded and developed the belief that everything in life would be better when I was finally included and adopted into a particular group of people. Feeling included and accepted has been among my deepest emotional longings—but I learned that having those needs met by picking from the options on the bubble sheet in order to keep peace and fit in wasn't the way to go about it. When I was a conservative, I felt the life force drain from my faith as I came to see the host of conservative beliefs, opinions, and attitudes that I in no way wanted to defend or participate in. When I first became a progressive, the same thing happened: I felt the vitality of my faith slip away as I grew to see some progressive beliefs, opinions, and attitudes that I also had no desire to participate in. The very thing I had wanted for so many years of my life—to feel part of a group—was now among the things I no longer believed, because that desire was rooted in fear. I no longer wanted to feel "in" with anyone if being "in" meant I had to limit my thinking or be less than the creative person God was inviting me to be. Instead, I found myself longing to be different from any of the options that had been presented to me—and to encourage others (that's you) to embrace this new way of living.

The key to rejecting the false binary options that the major camps in American Christianity present to us is found, I believe, in reclaiming the call to be "holy." I know for some that might be a trigger word. Growing up in rather conservative, fundamentalist circles, I heard about being holy a lot. In fact, as I write this, I can still picture the sweat dripping down some preachers' faces as they yelled at us by campfires about the need to be holy if we wanted to avoid hell's eternal fire. "Holy" had a very specific meaning for me growing up—a meaning that was burdensome in every possible respect and completely impossible to achieve.

Like many biblical terms we see in Scripture, the word "holy" and the call to be holy have often been co-opted by various tribes and adjusted to suit their particular agendas. In my experience, and perhaps this is true for you, too, the call to be holy has been a call to *conform*. Preachers tell us—warn us—that the Bible commands us to live holy lives (which is actually true), and then they prescribe for us all of the changes we need to make in our lives so that we'll conform to *the image and likeness of their particular brand of Christianity.* "Holy living," then, becomes a call to conform to the beliefs and practices of a particular group or tribe as evidence that we are truly walking with God. In other words, holy comes to mean that we pencil in the exact bubbles on the sheet that they tell us to, and the fear of hell, being wrong, or being on the outs with the group keeps us blindly doing it.

The sad irony of the way that holy living has often been misused to get people to conform to a particular Christian tribe is found in the meaning of "holy" when we look to biblical Greek: to be set apart or different. But when we read this word without our fear-based lens and sans Christian labels, we see something different.

When the Bible tells us to be "holy because God is holy," it's actually calling us to a beautiful *nonconformity.* Although we are called to be imitators of Christ, and to conform to his image and likeness, we must remember that his image and likeness do not conform to any of the various paradigms we like to use to box God in. Holy living, then, becomes conformity with Christ but *radical nonconformity* with all those Christian tribes or labels that try to neatly create a limited space where God supposedly lives and works.

Holy living, plain and simple, is an invitation to rebel against the preexisting religious establishments and politics of the current empire in order that we might become more like Christ—the one who does not fit neatly within those establishments. The less I believe in belonging to a particular American Christian tribe, the more I believe we are invited on a spiritual journey that has more freedom than we ever imagined, when we embrace the invitation to reject labels and false binary options in favor of learning to think in ways we have never thought before. The world tries to beg our loyalties to a conservative or liberal paradigm for understanding the world and how we interact with it, and our particular group tells us that there are only four options on our bubble sheet and only one of them is correct. But Jesus invites us to buck the entire system so that we can learn to be ourselves—people who think differently.

Now, a point of order for those of you who are feeling a bit defensive and may want to start policing some boundaries with me: reclaiming the call to be holy for people who have not conformed to worldly patterns such as the liberal-versus-conservative paradigm *doesn't mean that we just do whatever the hell we want and make up our own religion as we go.* That would be an equally perverted idea of being holy, and, worse than that, it would be idolatry. What embracing this invitation does do, however, is continue to free us to fully follow Jesus far beyond the boats and bubble sheets. We are free to embrace our own beautiful complexity as unique and individual image-bearers; we are free to love and affirm others; we are free to dream again and to both ask questions and suggest options no one else has. In short, we are free to be different wherever that leads us, even if that makes us a Holy Mischief Maker (which isn't so bad, really).

Since the modernist and fundamentalist controversies of the 1920s, American Christianity has been caught up in a battle between two false binary options—left versus right. Just as you and I are unable to fully grasp the significance of the teachings of Jesus outside of understanding the religious/political binary options of his day, we are also unable to fully appreciate our own role in God's story without stepping back and taking a good hard look at the religious and political climate we have been born into—a climate in which we might be unaware of and oblivious to the backstory. In this regard, you and I were born into a landscape that has been waging a hundred-year culture war where both teams are trying to suck us into taking sides and setting up camp with them. Because as humans we tend to have very narrow tunnel vision; we often find ourselves moving into one side or the other, believing the lie that the only correct options are the ones we currently see. Far too often, we fail to realize that *the entire system of binary options is bogus* and that sometimes the best answer is entirely rejecting the questions that are being asked.

Letting Go of Fitting In

If I could distill the solution to breaking free from the labels, breaking free from the false binary options we feel so forced to choose between, I'd summarize it as *letting go of fitting in*. And if there's one thing I've learned, it is precisely the letting go of fitting in—and all the smaller elements this may entail—that frees us to begin moving forward in meaningful ways into a new faith. Letting go of the belief that we need to fit in perfectly somewhere is the final, all-encompassing death that must happen before God can introduce us to a radical new life beyond fear. Every individual season of rebuilding faith is different, and each one has a funny way of leading us all to different places—and that sort of Christian diversity is good. When we no longer believe that fitting in is the end all and be all, we find the freedom to have faith that who we are is who God intended us to be—and who God intended us to become. If you're growing thirsty for a new, vibrant faith that will propel you to experience God in new and beautiful ways, letting go of fitting in, letting go of the fear of being holy, is a do-not-pass-go moment.

I will freely admit to you that I have no idea why God is a God who invites us into new life by first embracing death. All I do know is that (a) this *is* how he seems to do things, and (b) this *is* the process that brings the most life, as strange as it sounds. Apart from God, death is just death, but with God, death is a thing that can swell with life and ultimately give birth to something new and beautiful, something you never imagined would be born out of death.

Jesus taught his disciples this same thing, though he used the illustration of a plant that gives up its seed. Jesus explained it to them like this: "Very truly, I tell you, unless a grain of wheat falls into the earth and dies, it remains just a single grain; but if it dies, it bears much fruit" (John 12:24). As far as Jesus is concerned, there are two choices: hold on and remain a single grain of wheat, or let go to embrace death and thereby experience a life that is multiplied far beyond anything previously experienced or even imagined.

This is precisely what's so peculiar about the teachings of Jesus: the key to gaining new life is by first pressing through—and past—death in whatever form we find it. In this regard, letting go of the idea of fitting in isn't easy, but *it is certainly worth the effort*. I say this confidently, speaking as someone who has already experienced what can happen when we let death give birth to new life, and who can attest to what you'll experience when you let death become pregnant inside *you* as well. Letting the seeds produced by the destruction of our old faith fall to the ground and die is something that, ironically, will spring forth new life, just as Jesus promised.

Giving up on the idea of fitting in really isn't about quitting anything; it's more of an acknowledgment of what's true, a commitment to live within reality, and a way of opting out of a painful and destructive cycle of Christian living. In my own journey, I didn't give up on being a Christian, and I didn't give up on the commitment to participate in a local gathering of believers, but I did give up on the unrealistic expectation that I'd ever neatly fit into someone else's concept of what a "true" Christian thinks or what a "true" Christian does, or even what a "true" Christian believes. I want to follow Jesus—yes, the unaltered Jesus found in the New Testament—but trying to perfectly follow all the parameters of what this or that tribe says following Jesus looks like, especially as a precondition of acceptance, is just too exhausting for me. I tried valiantly, but I found that becoming a different kind of Christian altogether was a much better way of living.

It's important to point out that the concept of letting go of fitting in could be misused as an excuse to make up our own religion loosely based on Jesus, which would be another form of idolatry. But when we let go as a way of following *Jesus* instead of following *ourselves*, it is a beautiful experience. Essentially, the good and healthy version of letting go of fitting in is simply accepting the truth that living a life patterned after the way Jesus lived his (as we're told to do in 1 John 2:6) will lead to our always being less than a perfect fit within the religious and cultural establishments—*all of them.*

For me, understanding this perspective became a pivotal moment, inviting me to explore a spiritual path that has brought more life than anything I had ever hoped for. It came at a time in my life when I looked back and realized that my only hope to ever feel comfortable in my own skin was to accept that I was never meant to fit perfectly into a specific Christian category. As I slowly grew to embrace this, I began to discover that our individual uniqueness might be a *divine calling* instead of a curse. Continuing to force myself into various Christian tribes in the hope that I'd find a perfect fit was so futile that it potentially could have drained all of my inner resources and left me, once again, with nothing. These were limited and precious emotional resources—resources that I knew deep down I should spend in the pursuit not of acceptance, but of *Jesus himself*.

As I look back over the many years I have spent trying harder and harder to fit in, only to once again come to the soul-crushing realization that none of the circles on that bubble sheet represents me in all my complexity, I've started to see that our quests to fit in often follow the same pattern of consumerism. Those people caught up in the vicious cycle of consumerism are slaves to a cycle of always wanting and needing more. With each "more" that's acquired, there's a good feeling for a time—the appetite is rewarded. However, it doesn't take long for that appetite to grow once again, thrusting a person caught in this cycle back into the fast-flowing stream of needing that next best thing. The cycle continues endlessly, the person drains his or her financial resources and is left without ever having satisfied the original feeling that started the whole cycle.

While the desire to fit our identity or beliefs neatly into a Christian category isn't the same thing as unbridled consumerism, the pattern it follows certainly is. We often spend years bouncing from tribe to tribe, or label to label, or picking from the limited options on the bubble sheet, hoping that one day we'll fit in nicely without any tension. Along that journey, we have experiences here and there that begin to satisfy this inner longing to fit in, but the satisfaction we gain from those experiences is fleeting. And so we move on to our next big attempt to find a way to fit in—if not here, then somewhere over there. Many people will spend their entire lives spinning in an endless cycle that in and of itself can *never* bring fulfillment or satisfaction.

The most rewarding lesson I've learned about letting go of fitting in is that this is one of the key ways we can find and live in peace. Some applicable words from the Apostle Paul—words often not understood in their true depth—came to have new importance for me as I went through this transition of letting go. In the book of Romans he writes, "If it is possible, so far as it depends on you, live peaceably with all" (Rom 12:18). Throughout my life I had heard this verse multiple times in reference to church conflict (often a code word for me to zip it and get in line with the other insiders), but I had never once had someone encourage me to apply this verse *to my own being.*

You see, living at peace with everyone *includes living at peace with ourselves.* In order for us to be functional and effective followers of Jesus, and in order to work more harmoniously with others in this Jesus movement, we first must rid ourselves of those things that weigh us down, trip us up, and keep us from running the race set before us. It's easy and common to view such things as being external, but we must look at the *internal* things that trip us up as well. Letting go of fitting in becomes one of the ultimate ways we shed the key internal barrier to a more life-giving spiritual journey, and it is how we shed that which obstructs in order to make room for that which *propels.*

The constant need to fit in and the destructive cycle that it invites us into has always been an internal barrier, not an external one. It only feels external because it most commonly manifests in relationships with others. However, this battle of always wanting or needing to fit in is largely a battle within ourselves. As long as we are caving in to the vicious cycle of always trying harder in hopes that one day we won't feel like such an outsider, we are not being obedient to the scriptural principle of living at peace with ourselves.

Instead, we're living in turmoil, and that's not the life Jesus invites us to live.

We are invited to live at peace.

At peace with our neighbors.

At peace with our enemies.

At peace with God.

At peace with *ourselves*.

And that critical last part means we must be affirming—and not just to others who are different. We need to affirm that place inside us that desperately wants to hear that we are good, that we are beautiful, and that the ways in which we are different are gifts to be celebrated.

Letting go of the idea of fitting in isn't a way of rebelling against God, and it's certainly not pulling *away* from the invitation to follow Jesus. Finally letting go of fitting in means that we have found an area where we realize we need to trust that God is right. We're called to live at peace.

We're called to live at peace with others, yes, but that all begins by living at peace with ourselves.

This last big step is the one that brings the peace and freedom we have longed for. Letting go of fitting in, and the new life it invites us into, represents the true freedom that is found in Christ. This freedom is more than an abstract freedom. It's freedom to be who God made us to be, and freedom to become who God is *calling us to be.* Yet we can't get there as long as we insist on continuing the endless cycle of sacrificing the call to follow Jesus so that we can spin our wheels trying to fit in somewhere.

Becoming Human Again

Perhaps one of the most surprising benefits of not worrying about fitting neatly into a particular Christian mold is embracing our personhood. One of the most powerful emotions I felt during my crisis of faith was that of being dehumanized. As I looked at our bubble sheet A, B, C, or D approach to theology and identity, or our left-versus-right approach to secular politics, I realized that all my years trying to fit in to one of those circles on the bubble sheet had caused me to either lose myself or forget who I was. Whether I was lost or just forgetful, the net result was all that really mattered—and the result of that way of living isn't pretty. *Because when you feel like you lose yourself, you lose everything.*

When we accept systems that subtly tell us that we must fit into predetermined categories, labels, or any other way of being identified, we dehumanize all people—because human beings are far more complex than the words or categories we can think up in poor attempts to describe ourselves. This dehumanization is certainly something that we impose upon others—just think of all the times you read Internet commenters make generalizations about people, pejoratively calling them "liberal" or calling them "conservative," as if a single word can describe who they are or can help anyone judge whether they are good or evil (an action forbidden for the Christian to do). But when we participate in these black-or-white or us-versus-them systems, we actually dehumanize ourselves—more than we dehumanize others. Eventually we get to the point where we are not able to recognize the person looking back at us in the mirror.

When you live life convinced that the answers and options

on that bubble sheet are all there is, you sin against yourself by reducing your beautifully complex personhood to a small circle on a flawed test.

The truth is, my most recent spiritual crisis wasn't my first one—I've had a few over the years, of varying degrees. But this one was different because I began to develop some self-awareness and decided to respond to it differently. I realized that in previous chapters of wrestling, I was attempting to figure out who and what I was by looking at the options on the bubble sheet that had been handed to me. My searching, my wrestling, and my inner turmoil were always focused on trying to figure out which of the predetermined choices on that sheet best fit me—and I began to see how that had shaved away at my own humanity. To be fully human again, to be fully me, I had to reject the belief that any neat and clean category could ever define me—or anyone else, for that matter.

People are complex. I've never known anyone who was not complex, who didn't have a unique story of their own or who could be described in their human fullness with just a word or two. And yet, for some reason we attempt to do that—not just with others, but with ourselves. When we pick up that bubble sheet and look over the handful of options—the handful of words the world says we must use to describe who we are and what we believe—we deny our divinely blessed complexity and our own stories each time we try to make one of the words fit.

Take It from Finland—Get Rid of Your Bubble Sheets

A bubble-sheet approach to Christian living represents having to fit a mold, pick a side, and hold to one way of thinking. But

bubble sheets also have a cultural significance. I think one of
the chief reasons we Americans have a propensity to gravitate
toward the lazy form of thinking found in false binary options is
a byproduct or unintended consequence of some of our cultural
programming. We in the West live in a book culture as opposed
to an oral culture. As part of that cultural structure, the way we
understand knowledge is often linked to our ability to correctly
recall facts rather than wrestle with abstract concepts or engage
in abstract thinking. Those pesky multiple-choice tests are the
epitome of this kind of thinking. This standardized method
of testing knowledge simply measures our ability to correctly
recall and identify what we have already been taught is the
correct answer. This is how these types of tests work, and how
our culture measures knowledge; we are simply measuring the
ability to memorize. Unfortunately, this does not measure the
ability *to think,* which may be part of the reason why Americans
lag behind so much of the rest of the world when it comes to
education.

Finland used to understand and measure knowledge in the
same way, but that country became unhappy with the result. Its
school systems were chronically underperforming, placing the
country almost among the worst in the world, right next to the
United States. Unlike the United States, however, Finland decided
to overhaul its entire approach to education, basically throwing
everything out the window and starting over with some ideas
that seemed crazy to some people. It did away with homework.
It instituted more recesses. It insisted that rich children attend
the same public schools as their poor neighbors. It required
that teachers have more education before they could teach in a
classroom.

Instead of becoming the laughingstock of the education world, today Finland has the best public schools and the best educated children in the world. Finland is now the country to which other countries look when they want to learn how to improve educational systems and teach children well.

Oh, and Finland did one more thing: it got rid of most of those multiple-choice tests.

Why did they do this? Well, it's because Finland now places a higher value on teaching children how to think rather than testing their ability to identify a previously memorized answer on a bubble sheet. Finland wanted to teach its children to think more creatively, to think differently, to think deeply—and in doing so, it created the best public school system in the world.

Call me crazy, but I wonder whether Americans might learn something from what we've seen happen in Finland. Could it be possible that doing away with a bubble-sheet approach to the deepest questions of who we are, what we think, and what we exist to do might actually prompt us to think more creatively and to discover bigger and more beautiful things?

I think it might.

I believe there's a good chance that God is wondering where all the dreamers have gone and longs for people to step forward and dare to dream. However, we live in a world where nearly every political issue, theological issue, and social issue that we face is presented to us not as a problem or a question to ponder; it is presented to us with all of the possible correct answers already provided.

Bubble sheets and multiple-choice exams limit our thinking. They tell us what someone else believes the question is and what someone else believes the possible correct answers are, or are not.

There is no freedom of movement, no freedom of creativity—there's no freedom to be fully who God created us to be when we approach our spiritual journey in this way. Our journey is not for someone else to frame. It is not for someone else to list the *only* possible correct answers for us.

God created us for more. So much more.

I also believe that when we take this approach to what we believe and how we interact with the world around us, we unintentionally limit God. God certainly has a will and a desire for the world—and he has a will and a desire for our lives as well. But instead of God being a master puppeteer pulling strings behind the scene, or God having a master blueprint for our lives that will unfold exactly as planned no matter what, I believe God is one who allows stories to unfold in new and exciting directions via human partnership with the divine.

As Thomas Jay Oord argues in his book *The Uncontrolling Love of God,* God's central, immutable essence is love. At the heart of love is a refusal to coerce people against their will. Thus, God is a God who is partially constrained by his very love-essence in that he cannot force a story to unfold in a certain way; all he can do is invite people to align their wills with his and to partner with him to create and spread beauty throughout the world. In this way, we potentially limit what God can do in the world when we refuse to partner with him or when the only options we're willing to look at are the options that have been handed to us on that bubble sheet. Simply by using a bubble sheet, we unintentionally assume that God is limited in the possible questions, answers, and *even solutions.* Beyond limiting God, we also limit the ways in which we are willing and available to partner with him.

I believe that sometimes God is looking for a more creative

answer than A, B, C, or D and is looking to partner with people who have the courage and ability to think beyond the canned options the rest of the world is looking at.

Just like those old schools in Finland, Christianity has grown stale—and it might just be time to overhaul everything and get rid of those bubble sheets. Who knows? Maybe we'll begin thinking of different answers—or better yet, maybe we'll start asking a whole new set of questions.

So we have a choice: we can stay in these systems of false binaries and remain loyal to Christian labels, settle into groupthink, and submit to the pressures of tribalism. Or we can step out into a world that is far more difficult to define with words or categories.

When we no longer believe that we can or need to fit neatly within limited categories or options—when we say to hell with this bubble sheet and rip it to shreds—we reclaim our calling to be people who are different, who are set apart, and who embrace their divine uniqueness.

Some of the best advice I've ever received in life came from my friend Joe when I started my doctoral work. Joe plainly told me, "Your job is to see what everyone else has seen, but to think what no one else has thought." That advice stuck with me, even beyond completing my doctorate. It became a new way of seeing the world around me; it changed how I saw God, how I saw myself, and how I saw a host of other things. In the same way, I believe we are in desperate need of a new generation of Christians who look at the bubble sheet they've been handed and reject it entirely—freeing all of us to see what we've all seen, but to think what no one else has thought.

I knew that for me this was the only possible path forward—because trying to fit within this system suffocated my faith in every possible way imaginable. Part of me wanted to die inside, but more of me secretly wanted to live—knowing that living had to look different from what it had always looked like before.

I wanted to be free. I wanted to be creative. I wanted to be different.

I just wanted to be me.

8.

WHEN YOU HAVE FAITH ASS-BACKWARD

As soon as I broke free from the oppressive power of getting my identity from a Christian label, and as I systematically worked to resist the pull of camps, categories, and prepackaged answers, I began to find a new freedom in my new faith that I had never quite expected—and certainly had not experienced before. I was free to focus on the love of God, having repented of my fear of God. I was free to appreciate the Bible in new ways, having traded my Swiss Army knife view for that of a precise tool with a specific function. I was free to embrace myself, to love myself, and to allow myself to be loved again. I was free to dream of the future and all the beauty that can be imagined. I was free from small tents, big tents, and bubble sheets. I was free.

And I was absolutely, positively terrified.

Like, for real. It was like those first few seconds skydiving that were so terrifying I can barely remember them beyond the video that shows my eyes practically rolling to the very back of my head.

Being free, and finding a new, fresh faith wasn't supposed to result in this feeling, I thought. I mean, if this was all a journey into being unafraid, why the heck did I keep hitting these points where I was utterly panicked?

I found myself waking up each morning hearing the same question: "What if you're wrong?" I had been trained to instinctively ask this question during my youth—not about myself, because we had the full and undiluted truth (did you see what I did there?)—but I was instinctively taught to ask this question of other people.

When we went out "soul winning" as kids (which was essentially approaching people who weren't fundies and trying to save their souls in three minutes or less), we were warned that we'd encounter atheists, Roman Catholics, Pentecostals, and all sorts of other folks who were among the "lost." They had it "wrong." Of course, we expected all these people to reject our tracts, and to reject the "gospel" right along with them—though we hoped that some would come to the saving knowledge of Christ and say the sinner's prayer so that they wouldn't burn in hell when they died. Soul winning was always a mixed bag—you never knew who you'd run into.

While we certainly dreaded various types of false Christians, I think what we feared the most were angry atheists who were halfway intelligent or who had completed at least fifth-grade science. Those were the most difficult, because they wouldn't reject the tracts outright; they'd often take them, read them, hand them back to us, and then want to dialogue with us. It was a hopeless situation for a fourteen-year-old fundamentalist trying to save those damned souls before dinnertime, but one that was also like the holy grail of soul winning. If you could save an atheist who believed in evolution, you were getting really good at it and would probably become a legend among the other teenage fundamentalists. Such was the opportunity presented to me at an airport in Budapest when I was returning from a summer mission trip.

You would have thought we were all Mormons, given the blue slacks and skirts, white shirts, and blue ties we wore when traveling, but we weren't; we were your run-of-the-mill teenage fundamentalists who went out of their way to chat it up with folks at the airport in hopes of winning some souls before our flight. Just like Forrest Gump said, "If I was going somewhere, I was running," I was the kid who, if he was going somewhere, he was soul winning. Airports were great for that.

A few of my mates caught a good one on the line and called me over for the assist: a middle-aged atheist and science professor at a university back in the States, who had a beard and glasses to boot. Just as we were dressed for our part, he was dressed for his—and the game was on. Especially since my friends had called me in for the mission, I didn't want to let them down and knew this was my opportunity to prove to them that I wasn't simply the King of Bible Memorization; I was also about to prove I was the Master Soul Winner of the Budapest Airport.

So, I'll cut to the chase: the conversation didn't go very well. Turns out, this college professor was a tad bit smarter than the fourteen-year-old me; and since the totality of my knowledge on evolution came from a Chick tract, I had my work cut out for me. I knew that if I was going to be able to haul this massive beast in, I was going to need some additional time to reel—so I began praying that God would give me the seat next to this guy on the plane so that he'd be trapped with me for the next twelve hours, with no escape.

And what do you know? God wanted in on this action and gave me the seat next to the college professor. It was incredible, and as I sat down, I smirked, knowing that his sobbing in repentance before the throne was as good as a done deal. His blackened, evolution-believing soul was mine.

Apparently, he must have prayed to the atheist gods that he'd be seated next to me as well, because with a smirk of his own he took out a copy of *National Geographic* that had a monkey on the cover. He smiled as he unfolded the magazine and set it before me, pointing to the monkey and saying, "This is my grandpa! This is my grandpa!" The longer this kind of thing went on, the more I came to see that this guy wasn't just a Massive Soul-Winning Challenge—he was actually a bit of a prick. Realizing I had a feisty one on the line, I pulled out the big guns with a little help from my old friend Pascal: "What if you're wrong?" I asked.

You see, that's the question we young Christians were taught to ask the nonbelievers—the question that would make them consider the consequences of their beliefs and realize that if they're wrong, they might be headed straight to hell. It was my go-to question for many years after that failed conversion attempt and became a question that would come back to haunt me in my sleep during my faith crisis. I didn't convert the college professor that day, but the memory has stuck with me because I was so confident in that moment that I was right and he was wrong. Now, decades and a 180-degree faith perspective later, I lie awake at night asking that question of myself because that's the question I've always been taught to ask:

- What if I'm wrong about all this?

- What if God isn't nearly as nice as I'm now believing?

- What if the critics are right and I'm heading to hell, taking half of the people on the Christian Internet with me?

Finding a New Balance

It took a while, but I eventually did some inner work and realized where this question was coming from and why it troubled me so much. For my entire Christian life, the determination of who was in and who was out was made entirely by who believed the correct *things* about God (called "orthodoxy," meaning right thinking). As long as one had correct belief, one was in, but once incorrect belief started creeping in, it was a slippery slope to the fiery pit of hell.

When I became more of a progressive Christian, culture taught me that it wasn't so much right thinking about God that determined who was in or who was out, but right doing (called "orthopraxy"). On one hand, this was something fresh and beautiful. Instead of existing only in the mind and becoming stale, faith was encouraged to be lived, especially in the context of serving the poor, oppressed, and marginalized. However, this also left me with nagging questions in the night:

- What if I'm not doing the right things?

- What if I'm still unintentionally reinforcing a culture of patriarchy and white supremacy?

- What if the way I'm living is still somehow oppressing the poor?

- What if my language is continuing to stigmatize and marginalize certain groups?

- What if I'm still deficient in an area that God considers nonnegotiable?

- What if I missed something and I'm still screwed anyway?

They're all good questions, but for someone who grew up with such fear of God, deep-seated abandonment issues, and a nagging suspicion that at the final judgment God will reject me, a focus on orthopraxy over orthodoxy or orthodoxy over orthopraxy left me equally insecure. It was like the early stage of falling in love, where you know you're in love and your partner loves you, but you still have trouble actually believing it deep down inside. The fear that at any moment it could all be stripped away from you makes it difficult to be fully present, and unable to engage in true reciprocity and mutuality until you finally deal with the fear, and the root cause of it.

I had spent a good chunk of my life trying to figure out everything that was true about God so that I could think the right things. I then went on to a chapter of my life where I focused on all the right actions I should perform, which I hoped would prove that I was correct in the security that I had believed the right things. But both ways of living burned me out and drained the faith from my being—because to be honest, *I'm not good at right thinking or right doing.* At least, I'm not good enough at either of them to have any sort of confidence that God will one day find me acceptable. Furthermore, I realized that this struggle between orthodoxy and orthopraxy was another one of those false binary options, where maybe the correct answer is *both* and *neither,* all at the same time.

The critical importance of right thinking and right doing are both found in Scripture, so it's crucial to recognize that these aren't issues to be dismissed but to be explored and wrestled with. Jesus himself makes the case that both are a critical aspect of faith, at one point highlighting the importance of believing the right thing (John 3:16 and 11:25) while at many others highlighting the importance of doing the right thing (Matt 5:19–48 and 25:34–36). Thus, any version of Christianity that highlights one of these aspects to the exclusion of the other is certainly out of synch with Jesus—because Jesus highlighted both believing *and* doing.

On one hand, finding a balance between these two was important to me. I wanted to believe what was true (what corresponded to reality), and I wanted to do the right things (there's still a little boy inside me who longs to please and be accepted in exchange). On the other hand, I really needed to dig deeper and discover why I had so much anxiety around this— why I still, after all this time, had a nagging suspicion that God would never love and accept me . . . why I was a goat and *not one of the sheep.*

However, framing and measuring my faith journey by way of getting it right on one level or another wasn't working because it set the stage for me to live out my faith as *anything but* unafraid. More than that, it was actually discouraging me from even trying, because I knew I was destined for failure no matter which system I chose. The only real option for me to have any hope of spiritual survival was to stop believing that either orthodoxy or orthopraxy should be used as a measure of faith, of acceptability, or of lovability.

To move past this, I had to return to the concept of God's love and remind myself that love doesn't reject on the basis of technicalities or oversights.

Love Doesn't So Easily Reject

If random commenters on the Internet are right, I'm not only screwed, but I'm screwed because of a few technicalities. To the fundamentalist crowd, the facts that I no longer believe in a rapture, that I believe in the full inclusion of our LGBTQ brothers and sisters, and that I no longer believe in traditional teachings regarding hell demonstrate that I'm not truly "in." To them, God's love and God's acceptance depend entirely on whether or not we believe the right things—and not just central, core issues. A lot of folks are confident declaring people like me "out" over disagreements on issues that many other people would consider quite secondary theologically.

At the same time, plenty of progressive folks have issues with me, too, failing to have the grace to acknowledge that we're all at different stages of this journey and that we're all deficient in one area or another. Conservative Christians seem to have a piety like the teachers of the law and the Pharisees, while many progressive Christians seem to have the same form of self-righteousness— both sides police their tribes and often do so without mercy. This piety and lack of balance and grace are good recipes for creating a miserable person, which is why you'll find plenty of people who fit that description in both categories. When we ascribe to either of these extremes of measuring or judging others, we become tempted to think that God does, too—and this belief was one that I had to put on my list of things that I was no longer willing to believe.

What would it say about God's character if he sentenced us to an eternity of torture for getting a few things wrong? For some reason, we still hold on to this idea that God accepts or rejects us on the basis of an advanced theology exam. It is as if we still think at the end of time he'll dangle us over a burning pit and ask us questions about the consubstantiation of the Son with the Father, or he'll grill us on pneumatology as he decides whether or not to drop us into the fiery lake. While some people may reject this imagery, we function as if this is absolutely true each and every time we declare who is in and who is out on the basis of where they land on any given theological question rather than accepting the fact that some parts of their lives are still works in progress—imperfect and messy, just like the rest of us.

This doesn't mean that theology is unimportant. It doesn't mean that how we live is irrelevant. Instead, theology should help us explore our questions about God and let go of the idea that we're ever going to completely have all of our crap in one bag. This was incredibly helpful for me when my performance-based self-doubt arose, as it always did. I had to be unafraid and choose to believe that God was going to see my heart, see my desire to do right, see my desire to think right, and see all the places that I got it so totally and completely wrong—and love me *anyway*.

So, what if I'm wrong?

Well, I *am* wrong in many ways, I'm sure. And I *will be* wrong in many ways, I'm also sure. But I also came to no longer believe in the power this question once held over me—because I was convinced that God loved me not on the basis of my thinking right or doing right; God's love had to have its root *somewhere else*. In fact, I began to wonder whether I was using the wrong frame of reference entirely for viewing this new journey I was on and that perhaps it was time to set aside my focus on orthodoxy and orthopraxy in favor of something better.

Reframing How We View Our Journey

Here's a funny thing: When Jesus showed up on the scene of history, he didn't show up with an eighty-two-page statement of faith that he asked everyone to sign without reservations before they could be part of his crew. He didn't seek out the people who had their theology pretty tight (in fact, he was constantly arguing with this group), and he certainly didn't spend a ton of time with the people who had a pious view of their own right behavior, even if their behavior was *technically* right. Instead, Jesus sought out the people who knew they didn't have it all figured out—which is comforting for a person like me. The invitation he offered to them over and over was merely, "Come, and follow me." It was the simplest, but most profound, invitation ever—one we lose when we adopt the mindset that being "in" is anything more than being on a journey to try to follow Jesus wherever he leads us in our thinking or our doing.

During Jesus's life and ministry, the only distinction that ever mattered for an individual was whether or not he or she was trying to follow Jesus. The entire purpose of following him was to learn to become like him—the only possible standard we could ever have for what right thinking or what right doing looks like in the human context. The things that Jesus thought, and the things that Jesus did, were not a clean fit for those whose entire focus had been right thinking or right doing; Jesus was, and still is, altogether different and outside all of our camps and categories.

So, here's a crazy thought I had: Maybe the point of this faith journey isn't about a rigid pursuit of right thinking over right doing, or vice versa, but instead is a journey of striving to be more like Jesus in how we think and act—recognizing that it's a journey where we'll never fully arrive and that we'll always have some parts of it totally wrong. Maybe the measuring stick that really matters isn't whether we've perfected right thinking or right doing, but whether we're *moving in the direction of being more like Jesus* in the moment. It's a shift not in the ultimate goal, but in the thinking; it's a shift in reframing how we see both others and ourselves in relation to that ultimate goal of being like Christ. Instead of asking the question "What if I'm wrong?," I was beginning to ask, "What if this is just about trying to be like Jesus?"—which I found to be much more helpful.

One of the most common things I felt as I was trying to rebuild my faith was being spiritually and emotionally exhausted. I can't count the number of times I was so spent that I didn't know which way was up. From the earliest days of my childhood, I had this programmed *need* to know whether I was good or bad, whether I was in or out—a need born of the deep insecurity and the haunting suspicion that I was bad and out instead of good and in.

This deep insecurity followed me well into adulthood, leading to words of affirmation becoming my primary love language. I had a deep need to be constantly told that I was good; and I needed to hear such affirmations frequently, and in high doses, before I came close to *starting* to believe them. Of course, this insecurity played right into my old religious paradigm which told me that there were strict lines regarding who was in and who was out. No matter how I was able to parse that out intellectually, no matter what Bible verses I clung to with hope, I could not shake this insecurity. Feeling like we're out, we'll never measure up, we'll never be good enough, lovable enough, leads to a thirst that is nearly impossible to quench. For me, this unquenchable thirst meant that I had to change the way I was evaluating my spiritual journey—I had to learn how to see it through a different lens and learn how to ask myself a different question.

For me, finding a way to break free from this tug-of-war between orthodoxy and orthopraxy came by way of discovering the concept of bounded and centered sets, which has been articulated by an anthropologist named Paul Hiebert. Hiebert argued that many of us approach the Christian faith through what's called a "bounded set," which is essentially a grid-work of hard lines that determines who is in and who is out. For those of us who grew up in conservative flavors of Christianity, we answered the question "If you died tonight, where would you spend eternity?" via a bounded-set framework. People who believed or did X, Y, and Z were in; people who believed or did X and Y but rejected Z were out. Progressive Christianity can often operate by this same in-versus-out system of judging people. And this is precisely the type of framework that leads to our fear-based, nagging doubts as to whether we're acceptable to God. When we're taught that love will reject us on the basis of a technicality, we will always be afraid that *we* just happen to be part of that technicality.

Seeing the Christian life through a "centered set," however, presents us with freedom from fear and offers the affirmation so many of us long for. A centered-set framework isn't about in versus out but is about moving in a specific direction. To reframe our journey beyond the bounded set paradigm, we simply draw a circle and put the name of Jesus in the center—after all, this *is* all about Jesus and learning to be like him. The circle represents the wide spectrum of where we might be in life, and the center of the circle represents where we want to be moving toward; that is, we want to be moving toward Jesus. We want to be in the process of learning to love like Jesus loved and to do what Jesus did.

Or, perhaps we can frame it another way: if we believe that Jesus is the exact representation of the very essence of God (Heb 1:3), and if we believe that the central essence of God is love (1 John 4:8), we can draw a circle and write the word "love" in the middle. We can then begin asking ourselves a new question: "Am I moving toward love?"

This is precisely how we can reframe things to find freedom from those nagging doubts which tell us that we're totally screwed because we might have part of "it" wrong. Unlike the bounded-set approach where we're constantly trying to measure ourselves up to see whether we're in or out, the centered-set paradigm invites us to ask far more simple and profound questions: "Am I moving toward Jesus? Am I moving toward love?" If the answer is yes, then great! We're right where we need to be. If the answer is no, we probably want to recalibrate something in our lives so that we can change course. The difference is that this way of measurement isn't about being in or out; it's just about whether or not we are moving in the right direction.

I'm a huge fan of learning to ask better questions. Learning to replace our in-versus-out measurements with the question "Am I moving toward Jesus and love?" can be life-altering. If the point of Christian life is to learn to be like Jesus, and if we can answer yes to the question of whether we're moving toward a Jesus-emulating love, then it no longer matters where in that circle we may fall at any given moment—because as long as we're trying to move toward the center, *we're right where we're supposed to be.*

A New Way of Framing: Expanding Our Heart's Capacity to Love

Orthodoxy and orthopraxy are both important and are both things that Jesus spoke to, but I no longer believe that either of these things belongs in the center of our circles. I think that spot should be reserved for the exact representation of love: Jesus. By erasing my central pursuit of orthodoxy and orthopraxy and replacing it with Jesus, the essence of love, I realized that perhaps Jesus was inviting us to pursue something even better than right thinking or right doing: he was inviting us to pursue a heart that is constantly increasing in its capacity to love. If the Bible says that the opposite of love is fear, than living out unafraid is *really* about living out love.

Throughout his ministry, Jesus seemed far more concerned with the state of individual hearts than with expressions of right thinking or examples of right doing. From the squabbles we see Jesus engaged in, it seems obvious to me that he knew that a person can actually express right thinking and model right doing *without having a heart that loves rightly.* This is why he told some people that even though they were experts on Scripture, they had missed out on the key to life—which was him. It is also why he told others that their right behavior was meaningless, because inwardly they were like dirty graves. These people technically were thinking right, and technically, they were doing right—down to how they ceremonially washed their hands. But there is one thing they didn't do: they didn't cultivate hearts that were loving and thereby progressively expand their capacity to love. Jesus seemed to believe that a person can have right thinking and right doing and still not have right heartedness—and I think the heart is what he's *really after.*

Like right thinking and right doing, I realized from the onset that I'd never arrive at right heartedness *either.* Instead, viewing my faith journey through a centered-set approach gave me a life-giving and freeing sense of direction. With Jesus, the symbol of love, at the center of the circle, we can replace our striving for perfection with *a sense of direction.* True, I'll never be able to love the way Jesus loved; however, I can pursue a direction in life that focuses me on consistently expanding the capacity of my heart *to* love—a journey that naturally results in becoming progressively more and more like Jesus.

Jesus seemed to teach this centered-set approach to viewing life, though we often use some of the biblical texts to put forward a black-and-white, in-versus-out approach because of some nuance that's lost between ancient Greek and modern English. One English word that seems to trip us up and throw us into an in-versus-out approach to life is "obey"—another word that may be a trigger for some folks. Yes, at the end of his ministry Jesus certainly did tell his disciples to "obey everything I have commanded you" and to go and teach others to do the same. It is also true that going by English nuance only, it seems like this is a black-and-white, in-versus-out litmus test. When it comes to obeying, you either obey, or you don't—there's no middle ground. It's measurable, quantifiable, and absolute.

Thankfully, the Greek word is far less absolute than it appears in English. The Greek term found in these passages is a word that usually means "to keep or to guard." Without going deeper, the idea of *keeping* or *guarding* Jesus's commandments still seems like a pass-fail test—either you do or you don't. But I think that viewing it this way still misses the mark and some of the beautiful nuance that this word held in the ancient world.

I believe that "keeping" speaks more about focus than measuring success on a pass-fail basis. When we *keep* something, we hold it close to our hearts and allow it to progressively become our object of focus. The action of keeping becomes personal and intimate, not regulated by an outside authority. Whatever we keep becomes an object we love and cherish, and it becomes a center point from which the rest of our lives flow—like a compass.

The Greek word for "keep" also has connections to celestial navigation and "keeping the stars," which was impressively well-developed earlier than the time of Christ. In the ancient world, sailors used the stars to figure out where they were going and how to get there. By understanding the positions of stars in relation to one another, and by keeping their focus on those points in the sky, navigators were able to keep moving to where they needed to go. Certainly, traveling on the seas was no sure thing, but *keeping* the stars was one way to help ensure that they were at least moving in the right direction.

As any navigator knows, getting to your destination rarely involves a straight line; instead, most journeys have unexpected twists and turns. This is especially true for me, as I am what we call "directionally challenged" and can't seem to find my way to someplace even if I've gone there ten times. I don't keep the stars to find my way, but I do have a very special relationship with Siri. Before I head out somewhere, I tell her the address—which is the equivalent of telling her to "*keep* the address." As long as Siri *keeps* the address, I know that even if I screw up, she's still going to get me to where I'm headed—all she has to do is recalculate the route after I stray. Through a lens of navigation, then, we can see that "keeping" isn't about having a perfect, linear, or flawless journey; keeping is about having a *focus point* that you want to keep *moving toward.* Even though you may stray to the left or right, what matters is that you have an immovable object on the horizon throughout life—one that helps you "recalculate the route" when needed and to once again begin moving you in the direction you want to be headed.

Reframing it this way, we see that Jesus commanded those who would follow him to "keep" everything he commanded—that is, his commands should be at the center of our circles, and the only meaningful way to navigate our journeys is to point ourselves in the direction of his commandments and move toward them.

This, of course, begs the question, "What did Jesus command?" The answer to this question is quite simple: the commandment Jesus gave us was *to love* (Matt 22:36–40; John 13:33–35). Jesus didn't go around issuing dozens of random commandments.

He didn't hand out comprehensive theology exams that would determine who was in or who was out. Instead, Jesus told people that the most important thing they could do with their lives was to follow him and learn how to love.

Thus, Jesus himself invites us to draw a circle, to write "love" in the middle of it, and to begin walking toward that center as we experience ways to allow our hearts to love in deeper and more meaningful ways.

One of the biggest things I learned about myself during my journey to becoming unafraid was what a flawed and insecure person I am. This realization led me to see that trying to measure my spiritual success, health, or anything else by way of perfectly thinking right or perfectly doing right would make me feel worse, not better—because if something is a pass-fail test, I can assure you, *my name will be in the fail column.* I have no illusions about my name belonging anywhere else.

And you know what? I imagine that many of us feel this way. I doubt that more than a handful of us are narcissistic enough to believe that we truly do have it all together when it comes to right thinking or right doing. We are human beings. We are often frail and fallible, and we all arrive at the crossroads of a faith journey with our individual experiences, our hurts, our wounds, and our failures. This all means that we each live out our own unique mix of brokenness and beauty as we keep writing our stories. It also means that as long as we're using right thinking or right doing as a measuring stick to judge whether our stories are moving in the right direction, we'll be constantly stuck in front of a mirror that does little more than reflect all the things inside of us that appear broken and deficient.

I can promise you, we don't want to spend the rest of our lives in front of that mirror. Fear-based religion functions this way, the law that Moses wrote functioned this way—religion in general seems to function this way. But Jesus doesn't function this way. Jesus isn't a mirror that reflects back all the reasons why we totally suck. He's not a mirror that exposes all of our weaknesses, all of our brokenness, and all of our failures so that they can be thrown in our faces, leaving us with a sense of self-loathing and feeling like we can't get out of bed. Jesus isn't the guy constantly wagging his finger at us and pointing out those flaws that we didn't need pointed out because we were already hyperaware and ashamed of them. That's how it functions when we use these black-and-white absolute ways of judging ourselves—but that's not how Jesus functions. Not at all.

Instead, Jesus is the one who says, "Just keep walking toward me, and I will help you increase your capacity to receive and to give love."

When we strip away and shed off all the emotional rust that has built up from a lifetime of in-versus-out religion, and when we no longer believe that this is a healthy way to navigate or measure our spiritual lives, we are invited to return home to what we started out with before life took over. We're invited to simply return home to where our faith journeys began: Jesus.

There's No Place like Home

Toward the end of high school I became a restless soul who just wanted to break free, see the world, and find my identity (eighteen Maine winters should be enough for anyone to get stir crazy). It was a few years after my trip to Central America with my father—a trip that in hindsight altered the entire course of my life. We spent time hiking through the tropical rain forests of Costa Rica, went snorkeling at the second largest barrier reef in the world in the cays off the coast of Belize, and scaled the ancient Mayan temples of Tikal in Guatemala. As I stood atop Temple II at Tikal (you should stop and google a picture of that—but don't then check your Facebook page and forget that I'm here) and looked out at the dense forest that echoed calls of the spider monkeys, I knew then and there that Benjamin L. Corey was destined to break free and see the world. I had no idea how I'd see the world, but I knew that I'd let nothing get in my way.

After graduating high school, I did what good Christian children from my conservative New England Christian culture did: I set off to study the Bible at Word of Life Bible Institute in Schroon Lake, New York, for a year. Let's just say, the comment that Word of Life was a fear-based, rules-based place is an understatement. You couldn't date someone without a third party following to make sure you didn't hold hands; you were contractually forbidden to attend a "motion picture show;" and skirts shorter than knee length were considered to be the root of all evil. Oh, and you definitely weren't supposed to ask questions. I remember that part well. I—and this is something you probably *never* saw coming—was considered one of the rebellious kids. I didn't fully realize this until one of the Resident Advisors told me he had received a list of all those who had been identified as rebellious from the character reference forms our churches filled out before our arrival. I was pegged, but pegged for reasons that I'm kinda proud of now.

Although it seemed in many ways I was prepared for the fundamentalist culture I would experience—I had spent two summers as a teen on Word of Life mission trips—in fact there wasn't much that could have equipped me for the reality of living there. Most especially was the day-in, day-out drag of walking to my mailbox to collect whatever demerits I had amassed from violating one of the thousands of campus rules. After a few demerits, the administration would yank your weekend and assign you to labor, which they said kept tuition cheap.

My questioning the purpose behind some of the rules led the dean of men to accuse me of practicing witchcraft, saying that I was rebellious because I didn't accept his crazy notion that my parents transferred authority of me over to him (and he, of course, sat down with me and showed me in the Bible where it said "rebellion" was the same as witchcraft). It was a miserable few months, and it didn't take long for me to realize that whatever God looks like, God certainly couldn't look like *that*. In the end, my decision was easy: I became a proud Word of Life dropout after just one semester.

While home for Christmas break, I decided to take my destiny into my own hands. Benjamin L. Corey would go and see the world, and he found a way to get paid while doing it: enlisting in the military. It was the middle of winter, and the recruiter told me that odds were I'd get sent somewhere warm. I was sold. The funny thing was that this was the *one* true thing the recruiter told me. I was stationed in Del Rio, Texas—a place where we'd say, "This isn't hell, but you can see it from here." I was happy to get out of the north, but once I confronted military life in Texas, I realized the joke was on me.

And so that's how it all went down. By the time my folks had put away the Christmas decorations after ushering in the new year of 1995, I was on my way to "see the world," thanks to an impulsive teenage decision. Although in many ways I got more than I bargained for when I enlisted in the military, I nonetheless did get fulfill my dream—I saw the world. My near decade in the service included a seven-year stretch overseas that included Europe, the Balkans, the South Pacific, and the Korean peninsula.

On one hand, traveling the world was everything I had hoped it would be, and in many cases it was even better because I was able to live in new cultures, establish close friendships with locals, and experience depths of culture that one can't experience on a ten-day trip. On the other hand, however, seeing the world and serving in the military came at a high price on two counts: first, I slowly adopted a new nationalistic identity, and second, I suffered from chronic loneliness living alone and so far from home.

I created some amazing memories around the world during those years, but no memory compares with what it felt like to return home on leave. Most of my trips home were at the holiday season, so in addition to getting to see my family again, I was pleasantly confronted with the smell of roasting turkey and the joyfulness that radiates from everyone around what to me will always be the most wonderful time of the year.

My trips home were far more valuable than just visiting family. They also became a time when I was able to reconnect with the "me" who'd gotten so lost in my new military identity (the military tribe has a way of taking over nearly every aspect of your identity). No trip home was ever complete without taking a drive down to the ocean to sit on the rocks, listen to the waves, and just feel like me again. Even if it was frigid cold, sitting down at the ocean was something I had to do in order to center myself. Over the years I certainly missed my family, but I also grew to miss the truer version of me that got lost amid my shifting identity.

There's something powerful about returning home, setting aside the false elements of identity that beg our attention, and simply getting reacquainted with the reality that is always hidden somewhere beneath the surface. While visiting home on leave was a temporary opportunity to rediscover life without the competing loyalties of military life and individual identity, when I finally left the service permanently I was faced with a new challenge—one that not just required a revisit to my core identity but forced me start life over and rebuild it. Leaving my military identity behind required me to rethink everything about who I was and what my purpose in life was. So I took off my uniform, put away the combat boots, and returned home to start life over again. Fast forward a decade, and you get the version of me that you know now.

For those of us who are at a transition point in our faith— whether at the beginning, caught in the middle, or on the other side of deconstruction—sometimes we feel like our heads are spinning and we don't know which way is up. This can be discouraging and disorientating, even when we're beginning to be unafraid, even when we're able to see that naming what we don't believe anymore has a powerful ability to show us what we actually *do* believe. It is a process. It is a journey.

Once I reframed life by simply drawing a circle and putting Jesus in the middle of it, I came to remember that the best journeys of life end with a return home. Jesus was where my journey began, and even though the list of things I no longer believed was getting longer and longer (and will likely continue doing so), the one thing I kept coming back to was the fact that, for me, Jesus was home. A fascination for Jesus first led me to begin walking this path, and returning home to that reality was ultimately what would keep me on that journey.

At one point in the ministry of Jesus, things began to go downhill for him fast. Jesus had amassed a decent-size following, but many of them packed their bags and hightailed it, claiming that the stuff he was teaching was just too strange for them. After the room cleared out one particular time, Jesus turned to his original twelve disciples and asked, "So are you guys going to bail on me, too?" Peter, being the head disciple, answered for the group and essentially asked Jesus, "To whom shall we go to? You're the one who has the words of eternal life" (John 6:68).

This small band of misfits realized that out of every rabbi or religious leader they'd listened to, Jesus was the only one who seemed compelling to them. His words and ideas were the only words and ideas that seemed to be life giving. There wasn't anyone else on the radar who was remotely competitive, so stand or fall, they were committed to following Jesus, even if it seemed completely strange to everyone else around them. All these years later, Peter's answer still resonates with me and feels like something so many of us could say if we were asked the same question: Where else would we go? Jesus is the one with life.

From my experience and the many, many e-mails I receive from other parking-lot Christians going through a faith transition, most of us here in the church parking lot don't want to walk away at all. Good or bad, we've experienced enough to know that of all the options out there, *Jesus is the option that brings life.* And it's not *Jesus* who pushes us out into the parking lot, but the other BS that *wrongly gets attached to him.* He's the one whom we long to return to, minus all that other stuff.

Like those few disciples who refused to walk away that day, I, too, still find myself unable to walk away from Jesus. There's always been something about him that has fascinated me and kept me coming back for more. Even as a small child, I didn't dread church—I loved it. Even though it was a flawed space, it was the space where I found Jesus week in and week out.[1] Whether it was sitting in front of a green felt board looking at paper cutouts of Bible characters or listening to a compelling missionary speaker talk about how Jesus was working in a faraway culture, the whole Jesus thing never got old for me. Regardless of what bumps I've experienced in life, this man

Jesus still hasn't gotten old to me. I find myself perpetually drawn to him. I've never found life anywhere else, and that's *not* for a lack of trying.

Regardless of differences among us, I would venture to guess that most of our Christian journeys started with a very similar spark. Something about Jesus compelled us to say, "Yes, I want more of that!" Maybe for you it's easy to remember. For some others perhaps it's more difficult to sift through the dust of memories to put your finger on it. Either way, if you're a Christian, I'm convinced there must have been a moment when the person of Jesus seemed compelling enough for you to dive in and seek more.

Jesus, then, became our first spark—our first love, if you will—who invited us on this unpredictable journey. Somewhere along the line, however, negative experiences and heavy baggage within whatever Christian tradition or expression we fled eventually caused that initial spark to fade or die. Instead of Jesus at the center of our circles, instead of a focus on soaking up more of that thing that first invited us on this journey, we end up sidetracked and focused on a million other things that are anything but the one thing we actually wanted more of.

Life just kind of happens . . . to all of us. Jesus gets lost in the mix of it. I get it.

But Jesus—love itself—longs to be rediscovered, dusted off, and placed back at the center of our circles with nothing else occupying that same space. I was beginning to see that maybe chapters in life when God invites a transition in our faith are actually all about that—stripping away whatever fears that cause us to become less able to love, and less able to be like Jesus. Like a sculpture taking shape before my eyes, I slowly began to realize that what was emerging from the lump of clay was the same thing I started out with when I was just a little boy: it was the love I first saw in

Jesus—the love I began with, before everything got so royally screwed up.

It was the person I needed no fear of, but rather who was the perfect and ultimate expression of love. It was the person the entire Bible was designed to point us to—exactly what I had *thought* the Bible was about before the Bible became a Swiss Army knife. It was the Jesus of hope and optimism, the Jesus who had never known a tribal line he was afraid to cross, the Jesus who rejected prefabricated options and taught us to ask deeper questions, the Jesus who thought that even I might be worthy of receiving love not despite who I am but because of who I am. It was the Jesus who invited me to start this journey in the first place.

Stripping away my faith and naming what I didn't believe anymore had a strange way of leading me right back home to where it all began—the unique love that I once saw in the person of Jesus.

And with him at the center of my circle? It seems that's the key to truly living a faith that's unafraid.

9.

WHERE JESUS LIKES TO SHOW UP IN A STORY

Someone once told me that fear can best be described as an acronym for *Forget Everything And Run.* As I began to reflect on my journey of moving beyond fear-based faith and saying goodbye to my old relationship with God, I found this acronym to be as true as anything. But the funny thing is, I started to think that moving beyond fear-based faith isn't about moving *beyond* something, but instead is about *returning to* something that we had and knew all along. As we shed all the baggage and false beliefs that we have adopted and internalized, it *feels* like we're moving *beyond,* when we're really just moving *back.*

Trying to navigate my fear-induced spiritual midlife crisis felt like trying to follow a trail through dense fog. I hadn't been sure where I was going—I just knew that I couldn't stay where I was; I had to walk forward somewhere, because *anywhere* was better than where I had found myself. I never felt like I had a clear, linear path to follow—I was simply putting one foot in front of the other and walking forward the best I could. The discoveries I made along the way were divine accidents at best, and certainly nothing I can take credit for intentionally discovering. My journey had been random, but I don't think where I landed was random at all; I think I landed exactly where I needed to be: right back at the beginning.

I've long been a big fan of outdoor survival shows. There are few things I can watch without getting hopelessly bored during the first ten minutes, but survival shows are an exception. One of the key things I've learned from watching these shows is our propensity to walk in circles when we're lost and don't know where we're going. Certainly we've all heard the term "walking in circles" before, but when you're lost out in nature, this is an actual reality. The reason why we do this when we don't have a clearly marked path to follow is because most of us have a dominant foot that we unconsciously favor. Since we're unaware of this favoring, we tend to subtly take a firmer step on our favored side. Slowly, over time, this slight favoring of one foot over the other will cause us to walk in a full circle. In a physical survival situation this can be discouraging at best and deadly at worst, but in a spiritual journey—when our natural leaning is toward Jesus of Nazareth—accidentally ending up back at the beginning is life, not death.

Jesus—no matter how strange the place where we find him—is the salvation of our faith, not the death of it. As long as we are at least leaning in the direction of Jesus, somehow we'll make it back to where we belong.

What If There's No Such Thing as a Faith Crisis?

This entire journey began on the premise that I was having a crisis of faith. For those of us who grew up being taught that certainty and clarity of belief are at the heart of being a good Christian, waking up wandering through the fog—no longer sure whether we know what we believe—*feels* like a crisis. It feels like the opposite of everything we were taught we should experience on our faith journeys. It screams "doubt," "danger," and "crisis," leaving us feeling like our world is in upheaval and that God is somewhere beyond us . . . somewhere else. But what if there's really no such thing as a crisis of faith? What if we are simply misunderstanding what we call a "crisis of faith" and are framing it poorly on the basis of our limited understanding in the moment?

What if that moment of stumbling around in spiritual fog is actually the path to our salvation and not to our death?

What if it just *feels* like everything is going wrong, but really that instance is a moment when everything is about to going *right*?

What if what we often call a faith crisis is actually a divine journey—not *from* God, or simply *to* God, but a journey *with* God?

I am sure that although most of us begin our Christian journey because we are drawn to Jesus, we get held back by a religion that actually puts distance between us and Jesus. Sometimes, that religion heaps on rules, assumptions, cultural beliefs, and a myriad of other things that in time transform simply following Jesus into a complex religion that exhausts us instead of providing us with a vibrant life to be discovered and experienced. We are rarely conscious of all these things that are killing our faith because they become so enshrined in our belief system. And when we enter into an unexpected process of shedding off those things that we have grown comfortable with . . .

Well, that moment *feels* like a crisis. It *feels* like our faith is falling apart. It *feels* like everything has gone wrong. But I'm convinced it's not a crisis at all, but the birth of true faith.

I have begun to see that what we call a crisis of faith is actually an invitation by God to shed off all the things that are killing our faith. It's not a crisis or crash-and-burn moment at all, but one where God simply says, "I'm going to hit the pause button so that I can help you offload some of this needless baggage you've been carrying." The sooner we recognize what is happening and the sooner we recognize that God is inviting us into a rebirth of faith instead of the death of it, the sooner we're able to begin partnering with him in naming all those things we don't believe anymore, setting them aside, and walking forward to emerge from the fog.

For me, all the baggage I was carrying was deeply rooted in a fear of God, dooming my faith from the start. I had always been taught that the purpose of life was to have a "personal relationship with God" but also that the "fear of God is the beginning of all wisdom." No one ever taught me that there is no fear in love and that "personal relationship" and "fear" of any sort cannot coexist. Neither did anyone explain to me that when the Bible says "fear of God," it's not speaking of being afraid but simply of a healthy reverence for and awe of him. *That's* a memo that would have been nice to have been cc'd on.

In this way, the survival of my faith actually depended on having a faith "crisis"—because bringing my fear-based faith to a screeching halt and forcing me to take a good hard look at what I had been carrying was the only way to save my faith; it was the only way I would ever experience what Jesus called being "born again."

Wherever you might be in your faith journey, no matter how large or how small your crisis is, whether it feels like subtle discomfort or is world-shattering, let me tell you this: letting go of the toxic things we believe about God doesn't bring us to the end of our faith—it brings us to the *start* of it. It may feel dark in the moment, but I assure you, it is not the darkness of night, but the temporary, fleeting darkness that soon breaks into the sunlight of day. It is only when we become unafraid and name and set aside all those things we don't believe anymore, it is only when we say goodbye to the version of God we don't believe in anymore, that we finally see what our journey has all been about.

Saying Goodbye to the God of Fear

So much of my process of learning to become self-aware, identifying fear and the effects of fear, and trying to sort my life out took place in my counselor Joel's office. Over time I had grown more confident in our counseling sessions, even though I'd still frequently walk in, sit down, and say, "I feel stuck." In many areas of my life I had made dramatic leaps to the point where I was more and more often confronting fear and shedding it, but something occasionally held me back. Something I couldn't quite put my finger on.

Until one day, Joel helped me identify it when he commented, "You still haven't had your goodbye ceremony with God."

"Goodbye ceremony?" I replied.

"Yeah—that's what's holding you back. You may have identified a lot of things you don't believe anymore, but you still haven't officially ended the fear-based relationship you had with God. Until you do that, you're going to be prone to return to being stuck in scared, no matter how many gains you make. It's time for you to put a stop to all this so you can be free to move on. You need to end the old relationship you had with God so that you can start a new one."

He set two chairs facing each other, as if two estranged friends were preparing for a face-to-face conversation. Then he explained that one chair was for me and the other was for God, and the two of us were about to finally have a long overdue heart-to-heart discussion about everything. Joel told me that there's a healthy way to end relationships that promotes healing and closure and that this was going to be my only way forward if I wanted to finally say goodbye to my fear-based past.

Joel said the conversation that promotes healing has four parts: expressing what you regret, expressing what you resent, expressing what you appreciate, and expressing what you wish for the other in the future. In order to air everything out, in order to either say goodbye or begin a new relationship on a new foundation, a person has to say, in a healthy way, all of the things that linger in these four categories. Joel added that regrets were things we wish *we* had or hadn't done, resentments were things we wish *the other person* had or hadn't done, and appreciations were things that we'll remember about the other person and be thankful for. Finally, the ceremony ends with both people saying what they wish for the other when it's all over. In any relationship that's ending, or in a chapter of a relationship that needs to die and go away, each person has to have a chance to cover each of these categories and to express what they need to say so that healing, closure, letting go, and/or moving on can happen.

Obviously, since God hadn't shown up in the flesh to my counseling session, I would have to fill both parts in this conversation. But, Joel explained, this, too, had a purpose as it would force me to look at everything not just through my own eyes, but through the eyes of a perfect, loving father. The whole thing felt hokey to me at first, but I trusted Joel and decided to give the exercise—looking God in the eye and telling him my regrets, my resentments, and my appreciations—my best shot. But mostly that day I had regrets and resentments to get off my chest.

As soon as I began, I forgot that the chair I was facing was empty, and the scenario became painfully and authentically real for me. Although I couldn't see him, somehow, in a strange way, I felt that God was present in that chair.

And so, I looked at him and spoke what he had known was in my heart all along:

> I *regret* sacrificing so much of myself and making myself so miserable—all in an attempt to make you happy.

> I *regret* staying in situations that were painful and toxic for me—all because I was convinced it was the "right thing" and that it would infuriate you if I did anything else.

> I *resent* that you chose to have me born into a circle that taught me that I was supposed to be afraid of you.

> I *resent* you for sending so many people into my life who taught me lies about you.

> I *resent* having to spend so much of my life afraid that if I didn't love you back exactly the way you wanted, you'd throw me into a @#$%ing lake of fire.

I got a few more things off my chest, but when I was done airing my regrets and resentments, Joel made me switch chairs and do the almost unthinkable—speak for God. I sat there and imagined God as I knew him—a loving God perfectly revealed in Jesus, and listed what I imagined were his regrets, resentments, and appreciations of me. I tried to tap deep into my own heart and the corner of it that's a father, and I tried to imagine what I might say if that part of me were perfectly good and perfectly loving. Reflecting back on my own resentments and regrets, I began to speak:

> Ben, I *regret* choosing to have you born into a faith group that taught you so many lies about me and that persuaded you that I am someone you need to be afraid of. It's not true.
>
> I *regret* not doing more to keep your family intact.
>
> I *regret* not intervening in your last two adoptions, and that the last time you held your daughters Gracia and Janella was the final time you'd ever see them.

And then, I spoke what I imagined God had felt all those years that fear had created such a toxic barrier between us:

> But Ben, I have to be honest: I deeply *resent* that you thought I would actually set you on fire. It really hurt my feelings that you chose to believe that I was capable of doing that to you. That's not what I'm like at all—it's so outside of my character—and all those years you believed it were as painful for me as they were for you. I mean, would you set any of your kids on fire for not being able to always perfectly love or understand you? I'm hurt, and I resent that you'd think so low of me.

After God and I finished having our back-and-forth, airing our hurts and grievances, and even reflecting upon some of the things we had enjoyed about the first half of our relationship, Joel stepped in and coached us on how to bring the discussion to a close in a way that would promote our both being able to move on to something new. He wanted me to tell God, and God to tell me: "I don't know how long it will take me, but I want you to know that I'm willing to work on letting all this go and putting it behind us." The words didn't come easy, but it seemed like God and I were two people on the verge of divorce who listed all the reasons why

the marriage should end but who then broke down in tears at the
end of the discussion, each owning their own part and agreeing
to change and give it another shot—but acknowledging that
everything had to be different this time.

Moving forward, I wanted to be able to pull close to God
without worrying that he'd always be looking for a reason to smite
me, without worrying that somewhere in a closet he had secretly
stashed a can filled with gas so that he could douse me and set me
aflame when I was sleeping and unsuspecting. I couldn't move
forward with a relationship believing he was like that. It's like what
my friend Matt once said: "If there is a God, and he requires you
to follow certain rules, regulations, and routines in order to gain
his favor, then he's a petty asshole who's not worth your time." I
desperately wanted a relationship with God, but it couldn't be the
old relationship I was saying goodbye to, because that one didn't
work—I never would have measured up, no matter how hard I
tried. And plus, that guy just scared the daylights out of me.

I imagined God wanted things to be different moving forward,
too—because there's no way our old relationship worked for him,
either. I imagined that maybe he sincerely wanted me to live fully
and freely, that maybe he wanted me to embrace everything he
made me to be, to embrace all my experiences that led me to this
new horizon I was moving toward, and that maybe even he wanted
to see what an emotionally intimate relationship could be like if
we didn't build the entire freaking foundation on fear. I realized
that God, too, wanted the two of us to move beyond a fear-based
faith—because what he was really after all along was just intimacy
and being given the gift of seeing and loving me fully, just as I was.

And so, on that day, God and I decided to say goodbye to the
way things had been between us for so long. We agreed to move
beyond the fear-versus-performance framework, and we agreed

to do our best to let go of our regrets and resentments so that we could be free to finally move beyond a fear-based faith, together.

The Part of the Story Where Jesus Shows Up

This book has been about me, but I wrote it for *you*. I thought about you every single day that I labored over these words.[1] I've read your e-mails and your comments, and I've talked to you at festivals and universities; and those faces and stories of individuals wrestling with letting go of their old beliefs were with me at every turn. And what I know about you is this: your journey, although full of nuance and individual complexity, is far more like mine than it is different. Many of us—I dare say most of us—grew up simultaneously being drawn to Jesus but being scared of God. That fear, whether we knew it or not, became the foundation of our faith and permeated every aspect of our lives—sometimes overtly, sometimes subtly. This fear is sold to us as our friend—someone sent to help us avoid really bad things—but that "friend" has a way of making a mess of our lives, because fear is a friend operating with minimum information at best and is an outright liar at worst. Hang around this friend long enough, and you'll face the classic choices: deny reality or dismantle the whole machine and see what's left when you're done.

I think many of us coming from fear-based backgrounds who experience the type of crisis of faith I've processed in this book resist the only journey that can free us to a true rebirth of our faith because we're afraid. We're afraid that we'll have to walk through it alone. We're afraid that naming those things we don't believe anymore will lead to the death of faith instead of the birth or revitalization of it. We're afraid of countless things that hold us back from the journey we most desperately need, but equally dread. We get caught up into all these things, get dizzy in our spiritual fog, and do a whole lot of goin' nowhere. Let's be honest: I'm not the only one who gets stuck in scared.

I wrote this book because I don't want you to be stuck in scared any longer than you already have been. Maybe some of you have a keen awareness of the way fear tends to drive every aspect of our faith, the way it has distorted our view of God, and the many ways that fear takes hold and begins to strangle us. Perhaps others of you are just at the early stage of catching on, or maybe even others are still caught in the cognitive dissonance of believing in a loving God who is going to set you on fire if you don't get the relationship right. I gave a year of my life to this book for one reason: no matter who you are or where you are on the spectrum, I want to invite you to be unafraid.

Becoming unafraid is a journey, and like I warned you at the beginning, the start of the journey—whether you sought it out or not—is certainly scary. I think we have a tendency to resist purposefully shedding aspects of old beliefs because there is a degree of comfort in sticking to what we know, settling and adapting to the way things have always been, even when we have a hunch that something out there is better. The invitation to become unafraid is an invitation to take a risk—to usher in a chapter in your spiritual life where you consciously name all those things you're keenly aware you don't believe anymore, and to invite God to help you discover what you *do* believe as a result. Not only do I believe that this process is good, helpful, and necessary for a vibrant spiritual life that leaves us unafraid, I think the moment we embrace what appears to be a faith "crisis" is the exact moment that Jesus loves to show up in a story.

Jesus's death on the cross was the ultimate blow to all of his disciples, and he had a good number of them beyond just the twelve we usually speak of. When we read the story of the life of Jesus, we already know how it ends, but those who lived when he lived and followed him experienced all those things in real time and did not have the big-picture understanding we have. Even though Jesus had predicted his death many times, the disciples never seemed to grasp what was about to happen, and when it did, it was a major shock to their systems. In fact, it destroyed their whole world—three years of hopes and dreams were dashed in fewer than twenty-four hours.

No one has experienced a crisis of faith quite like what the disciples experienced after the death of Jesus. For the first time, they were scattered. They were disillusioned. They were afraid. More than anything, they immediately had to wrestle with the reality that everything they had believed no longer felt true. Jesus being crucified had never been part of the plan, and when it happened, their world was shattered.

The disciples had no other alternative than to embrace the end of all they had believed and all they had hoped for. However, their limited view of reality was not ultimate reality, because when God is involved in a story, *death is never the end but is always the gateway to rebirth and resurrection.*

In the book of Luke, we're told that on the day of Jesus's resurrection, two of Jesus's followers are walking down a path toward a town called Emmaus when Jesus walks up beside them on the trail. Luke says that the two men are "kept from recognizing him" and walk and talk with him having no idea they are walking and talking with the resurrected Jesus himself. Their fear and depression after Jesus's death permeate them, so Jesus asks them why they seem so despondent. One of them, perhaps annoyed by the question, replies, "Are you seriously the only person in this city who doesn't know what just happened this weekend?" They then go into what I imagine was a long explanation, listing for Jesus all the old beliefs they had and why they no longer believed them.

You see, like the crisis of faith so many of us experience, it wasn't true that the disciples didn't know what they believed anymore—they were just keenly aware of some things they no longer believed. As they stepped out in courage, as they named those beliefs out loud and became honest with themselves about what they no longer believed, we find Jesus showing up in the story.

As Jesus walks with them, we're told that he starts at the beginning of the Hebrew Scriptures and explains that the entire story of the Old Testament was a story designed to point to him and that everything that did happen was *supposed* to happen. He essentially explains that their faith crisis isn't a crisis at all and that the death of old beliefs is something that can give birth to a new faith that is beyond anything they can imagine—or that we can imagine. Becoming unafraid to name the things we don't believe anymore opens our eyes to the new things God is doing in ourselves and the world, and has a way of leading us to discover what we truly *do* believe. For these disciples, what they thought was a crisis of faith was really God leading them to shed some false beliefs they had long held about God and to become willing to see, embrace, and experience a deeper reality—one where there's no need to be anything but unafraid.

I believe that you and I are not that much different from these disciples who were walking on the road to Emmaus and who reached a point in their faith journey where shedding old beliefs was no longer something they could delay. I believe the place we find ourselves is not random and devoid of purpose but is a necessary and beautiful part of our journey if we'll embrace it for what it is and let Jesus show up at this crucial part of our story. I'm convinced that he will show up—because this part of the story seems to be Jesus's favorite place to do just that—and when he does, like on the road to Emmaus, he will help us reflect on where we've come from and help us see that what we thought was a crisis of faith is actually about something much bigger.

When I Realized It Was About More Than Just Being Unafraid

During the year I was writing this book, I spent countless days just sitting with my story. Some of them were good days, and some of them were really heavy and painful days. My road to Emmaus was a long and lonely one.

But if we have the courage to keep walking forward through what *feels* like a crisis of faith, we will eventually find new life— because a faith crisis is really just an illusion where new life comes to us temporarily clothed in death's garments. Like one of those optical illusions where there is a hidden picture within a picture and you have to relax your eyes and free your mind so that you become able to see the hidden picture just beneath the deceptive exterior, a crisis of faith is often about something deeper than we realize. It is not necessary to see it, or even understand it, while we are walking through it—we just have to keep walking forward and trust that Jesus will show up when we most desperately need to understand the meaning of the journey we're on. Although I had long realized that my journey was one of becoming unafraid, when Jesus finally showed up in full force in my story, it was like a road to Emmaus moment where Jesus invited me to reflect back on everything so that I could see what I had always seen—but this time think what I had never thought.

The hidden reality Jesus showed me was that learning to be unafraid is more than simply shedding fear; becoming unafraid is a journey of learning how to expand our capacity to love, and to be loved.

To be unafraid is to love.

Every single belief I had shed, each and every belief that I looked in the face and defiantly refused to believe anymore, was a belief getting in the way of *love*. And as I've said already, when the Bible describes the opposite of love, it doesn't describe hate—it describes *fear*. Yes, my particular journey was centered on letting go of fear and watching what changed as a result. But the deeper reality is this: becoming unafraid and moving beyond fear-based faith isn't so much about being freed *from* something as being freed *to* something. What it truly means to be unafraid is that we have been freed to love and to be loved in ways we once thought impossible.

My view of God was hopelessly distorted by fear, making intimacy and the free exchange of love impossible. Believing God was capable of doing what an ISIS terrorist would do may have been what I was taught growing up, but that's not the foundation of a loving relationship. Once I embraced the fact that I was wonderfully made and had unsurpassable worth in God's eyes, so much so that he wouldn't dream of setting me on fire, I was finally free to enter into a new relationship—one that was founded on love, not fear.

My approach to the Bible was causing me to miss its central invitation: to follow in the footsteps of the one who came to earth in order to perfectly demonstrate love. Disbelieving that the Bible was a Swiss Army knife where everything was on equal footing and rejecting the idea that God could be both the Puppy Slayer *and* the Word made flesh who commanded we love our enemies freed me to focus on Jesus, the one who can expand my capacity to love.

The inner beliefs I had adopted about myself—messages that were damaging and grossly untrue—had made it nearly impossible for me to love myself or to allow myself to be seen and loved by others, including God. As God invited me to look at each of those lies I had adopted as truth, I was finally free to be loved for who I am, not despite who I am. I was free to embrace the truth that we are created by love, in the image and likeness of love, in order to give and receive love.

The negative view I held about where God's story was heading had caused me to adopt an outlook of pessimism instead of hope. This led me to become unloving by way of passivity, because it required nothing of me in the moment. Yet, as I shed that belief, I was free to become a dreamer again—a person who spreads love and who makes the world a little less broken.

My participation in Christian tribalism had caused me to become extremely unloving to anyone who did not share my particular label at the time. My identity had become so packaged and defined that I had robbed myself of the ability to increase my capacity to love those outside of my own theological boat. Yet, with each belief I shed in this area, I was free to look at everyone around me and to find reasons to love them, regardless of what label they wore or didn't. More than that, I was able to see how Jesus—the ultimate expression of love—was always on the horizon inviting us to partner in something new that he's doing in the world—and that something is *always* loving.

My bubble-sheet approach to Christian living had profoundly stifled the degree to which I could love and how creatively I could love others. When we are locked in rigid ways of thinking and when we allow others to constrain which answers we come up with, we severely limit love. Sometimes love is traditional, sometimes it pushes controversial boundaries; love, by nature, comes up with new and creative answers, and sometimes love even rejects the questions asked in order to formulate better ones. Throwing away the bubble sheet and our No. 2 pencils frees us to love more creatively.

My in-versus-out approach to the Christian journey—one that was measured by either right thinking or right doing—had completely sidetracked me from my ultimate purpose of living. Instead of expecting me to rigidly focus on getting my theology right or getting my behavior right, God really wanted me to focus on moving in the direction of Jesus, which naturally expands our capacity to love. He wanted me to write the name of Jesus in the center of my circle and spend my life moving toward him—the ultimate expression of love.

And that's when it clicked. That's when I looked back and saw that I wasn't *beginning* a journey in the direction of love—*I had been on one all along.*

Everything that I experienced during my crisis of faith—every belief I had shed—was a belief that was getting in the way of love. And with each belief I shed, I began walking deeper in the reality that I was created by love, in the image of love, to receive and reflect love—and that everyone else is, too.

The willingness to join Jesus, the willingness to have the courage to name the things you don't believe anymore and say goodbye to them, the willingness to see the new thing God is doing in your life and in the world, and the willingness to expand the capacity of your heart to give and receive love is what this journey is all about.

To begin, all you have to do is look fear in the face.

And then rebelliously "un" it.

ACKNOWLEDGMENTS

I wrote this during a challenging year in my life. In fact, looking back, I'm not sure how I managed to write it. Undoubtedly it is in large part because of friends and colleagues who have encouraged me, checked in on me, and reminded me that there is still goodness and beauty in the world, and because of people who rallied around this book and wanted to see it become a reality. It would be impossible to thank everyone individually without accidentally missing someone, but I'll give it a try.

To Tracy, Julissa, and Johanna (okay, and Saige): How could one express what we've been through together, and all the things that I am grateful for as I look back on our story, in less than a few sentences? I don't know the answer to that. So instead I'll simply say, "Thank you for all of it," because I believe that every chapter has elements of hope and beauty that wouldn't exist or one day be discovered had our story been written any other way.

Nothing happens without a good agent, and I could not be more honored to thank Greg Daniel for being mine. I deeply appreciate our talks, his insight and wisdom, and his directly telling me when I had an idea that sucked.

To my editors, Mickey Maudlin, Anna Paustenbach, and Jessie Dolch, thank you for the vision of what this book could become and for an editing process that pushed me and helped me become a better writer.

To my family: thank you for all you have done over the years and the many ways this life journey has been richer because of you.

For friendship, encouragement, support, prayers, random texts, or asking how you could support or encourage me over this past year, I offer my sincerest love and thanks:

To EVERYONE in Secret Facebook Group, most especially those of you who blew up my phone with encouraging text messages when I was at my darkest moments. I won't mention you all by name because, well, then the group wouldn't be much of a secret anymore, but know that I love and appreciate all of you. Especially on birthdays.

To all the folks in the Undiluted Community Group—you make me proud. Thank you for turning an online experiment into a beautiful place of support and encouragement.

To Joel, thank you for being part of my journey and helping me realize it was all about fear—and thanks for the absolutely weirdest metaphors I've ever heard in my life (I thought you were here for the hunting?).

To Kristen Howerton, Chad Markley, and Paul Martin, thank you for your encouragement and wisdom.

To Matthew Paul Turner, thank you for being a loyal and trustworthy friend.

To Rogier van Bakel, thank you for your years of friendship and for hopping in your car and driving across half the state just to cheer me up.

To the Jordan crew, who reminded me that colleagues can also be really good friends: Jamie Wright, Zack Hunt, Kerry Connelly, Christian Piatt, MPT, and Jana Blazek, thanks for what will be lifelong memories and friendships.

To those who randomly checked in on me at some point on the journey and helped me remember that I wasn't alone, even if it felt that way. I didn't always have the emotional energy to respond, but I want you to know I appreciate your checking in, as simply feeling remembered by you often gave me the courage to write: Brian and Peri Zahnd, Bruxy Cavey, Shane Claiborne, Frank Schaeffer, Ken Wytsma, Thomas J. Oord, Reba Riley, Micky Jones, Kurt Willems, Kristi Dale, Carrie Ann Chesney Dressler, Erin Albright, Meg Munoz, Nate Pyle, Kimberly Knight, Justin Shumaker, Joy Bennett, John Berry, Andrew March, John McGarry, John Pavlovitz, David Henson, Mark Sandlin, Matt Young, John Shore, and Trey Pearson. I'm sure I forgot someone, but wow, just writing out those names reminds me that I am beyond lucky to have people in my life like you. Please forgive me if I was out of it and didn't reply, or replied cryptically—just know that I kept track and remembered each one of you.

Of course, to the readers out there who have given me the tremendous privilege of walking with you, encouraging you, and sometimes messing with your long-held beliefs, thank you for the honor of being part of your journey. You have also been part of mine, and for that I will always be grateful.

NOTES

Chapter 1: A Spiritual Midlife Crisis

1. "Jordan Vows Harsh Response to Pilot's Killing by ISIL," *Aljazeera*, February 4, 2015, http://www.aljazeera.com/news/middleeast/2015/02/jordan -vows-harsh-response-pilot-killing-isil-150204025337518.html.

2. My wife and I adopted four children over the years—two from Peru and two from the Democratic Republic of Congo. One of our daughters had needs that ultimately required long-term residential therapy, and our daughters from the Congo were some of the Congolese children who got permanently stuck in country due to strife in the Congolese government. If you haven't followed me over the years, you can read more on my adoption journeys at my blog: http:// www.patheos.com/blogs/formerlyfundie/category/adoption-2/.

3. This process was Imago Therapy, which is a specific theory of counseling that helps identify and heal childhood wounds.

4. Historical theorists have described the fear responses as "fight or flight," but some are now arguing that there is a third category: "submit."

5. All apologies to my Swiss readers—Switzerland is actually one of my favorite places in the world.

6. See Episode 36 at https://thatgodshow.podbean.com/.

7. See 2 Timothy 1:7.

Chapter 2: The God I Just Couldn't Believe In Anymore

1. John 15:15: "I do not call you servants any longer, because the servant does not know what the master is doing; but I have called you friends, because I have made known to you everything that I have heard from my Father."

2. You can find this quotation, along with inspiration and insight, in Frank Schaeffer's book, *Why I Am an Atheist Who Believes in God: How to*

Give Love, Create Beauty and Find Peace (North Charleston, SC: CreateSpace, 2014).

3. Peter Kreeft, *Knowing the Truth About God's Love: The One Thing We Can't Live Without* (Ann Arbor, MI: Servant, 1988), 91.

Chapter 3: When the Word of God Isn't What You Thought It Was

1. Don't listen to my critics. I love the Bible today every bit as much as I did when I was still a fundamentalist; I just love it *differently*.

2. Peter Enns, *The Bible Tells Me So: Why Defending Scripture Has Made Us Unable to Read It* (New York: HarperOne, 2014).

Chapter 4: Discovering You're More Than Just a Sinner

1. The original song says, "*when* there is nothing good in me," but at our church the given lyrics simply said, "there is nothing good in me." The various versions on the Internet indicate that our church wasn't the only one singing this alternative version.

2. The term "Shalom" refers to an individual or situation being in a state of wholeness, where everything is as God originally intended it to be.

3. Thomas Jay Oord, *The Uncontrolling Love of God: An Open and Relational Account of Providence* (Downers Grove, IL: IVP Academic, 2015), 161.

4. I delve deeper into shalom and these categories of shalom in my doctoral dissertation "Blessed Are the Shalom-Makers: Toward a Shalom-Focused Human Trafficking Aftercare Social Movement," Fuller Theological Seminary, 2016.

Chapter 5: Ending the End Times Narrative

1. Stephanie Samuel, "Rapture Prediction to Devastate Christians' Faith?," *Christian Post,* May 20, 2011, http://www.christianpost.com/news /rapture-prediction-to-devastate-christians-faith-50351/.

2. Samuel, "Rapture Prediction."

3. "Robert Fitzpatrick Reacts to World Not Ending," *Huffpost,* May 23, 2011, http://www.huffingtonpost.com/2011/05/23/robert-fitzpatrick-may-21 -2011_n_865483.html.

4. http://www.independent.co.uk/news/world/americas/tricky-reality-for -preacher-after-world-fails-to-end-2287701.html.

5. For information on Darby, see LeAnn Snow Flesher, "The Historical Development of Premillennial Dispensationalism," *Review and Expositor,* vol. 106 (Winter 2009).

6. John Nelson Darby, "Progress of Evil on the Earth," in *Collected Writings of J. N. Darby, Prophetic 1,* at BibleTruthPublishers, http://

bibletruthpublishers.com/progress-of-evil-on-the-earth/john-nelson-darby-jnd
/collected-writings-of-j-n-darby-prophetic-1/la62221.

7. Rebecca Leung, "The Greatest Story Ever Sold," *60 Minutes,* April 13,
2004, http://www.cbsnews.com/news/the-greatest-story-ever-sold/.

8. "Pastor John Hagee Net Worth," Celebrity Net Worth, http://www
.celebritynetworth.com/richest-celebrities/authors/pastor-john-hagee-net-worth/.

9. Nate Pyle, "Why Mark Driscoll's Theology of SUV's Matters," May 3,
2013, http://natepyle.com/why-mark-driscolls-theology-of-suvs-matters/.

Chapter 6: Following Jesus Instead of the Tribe

1. While Mike had an obvious concern for my ability to make good choices
and live out Christian values, in hindsight I wish he had applied that same
passion for Christian living to himself. In 2001 he was convicted as a serial rapist
whose victims ranged in age from sixteen to seventy-five. The judge said the
life sentence was due in part to his lack of remorse and the violent nature of his
crimes. http://www.seacoastonline.com/article/20011208/News/312089986.

2. For when one says, "I belong to Paul," and another, "I belong to Apollos,"
are you not merely human?

3. Jen Hatmaker, "My Saddest Good Friday in Memory: When Treasured
Things Are Dead," April 14, 2017, http://jenhatmaker.com/blog/2017/04/14
/my-saddest-good-friday-in-memory-when-treasured-things-are-dead.

Chapter 7: Faith Doesn't Come with a Bubble Sheet and a No. 2 Pencil

1. This isn't to say that Jesus never took sides in some of the debates of his
time—he did. We often find him in agreement with Hillel, except when asked
whether he agreed with Hillel's extreme leniency on divorce that allowed a man
to send his wife into destitution over something as trivial as being a bad cook.
In that case, Jesus disagreed with Hillel and took a radically pro–women's rights
position.

Chapter 8: When You Have Faith Ass-Backward

1. I believe this is the one major downfall of all of our critiques of
fundamentalism: we forget that for all its flaws, we *still* found Jesus there, and I
for one am grateful.

Chapter 9: Where Jesus Likes to Show Up in a Story

1. I wrote much of this book during the summer months while sitting on the
banks of Lake Auburn in Maine. Many days as I struggled with my thoughts and
words, I sat there on the shore of the lake and prayed for you.